USING LESS STUFF!
STUFF!

Helping schools and businesses
save money!

USING LESS STUFF!
First published in 2014
Writing Matters Publishing
30 Longbridge
Ashford Kent UK TN24 0TA

info@writingmatterspublishing.com
www.writingmatterspublishing.com

Design by Writing Matters Publishing
Cartoons by Andrew Priestley

ISBN 978-0-9575440-2-4

Please Note: This book is intended as information only and does not constitute specific cost reduction advice unique to your situation. The Author, Publisher and Resellers accept no responsibility for loss, damage or injury to persons or their belongings as a direct or indirect result of reading this book.

Dedicated to all those who have helped me get from where I was to where I am now.

Testimonials

BERKHAMSTEAD SCHOOL

"Berkhamsted School has worked with *The Cost Reduction Company* on a range of projects including cleaning services, photocopying, telecoms and waste management. Their advice and industry expertise has helped us to reduce costs, to become more efficient, to introduce green initiatives and to get independent confirmation that we are already conforming to best practice. We have found their approach to be flexible and tailored to the project so that it best suits our needs, and their help to be pro-active and value added, whether or not in the end we have switched suppliers."

Peter Nicholls, B.A. (Hons)
FCA Vice Principal (Business Operations)

BRADFIELD COLLEGE

'Bradfield College is a co-educational boarding school for 13–18 year olds. It is important to Bradfield that its overheads and costs are managed as efficiently as possible, so that its resources are focused on the education of its pupils. Bradfield has worked with *The Cost Reduction Company* over a number of years, during which time they have saved us significant sums. As Bursar, I would recommend them to other schools and would be willing to provide a reference.'

Trefor Llewellyn
Bursar, Bradfield College

BROOK HOTELS

"We asked *The Cost Reduction Company* to look at our existing wines, spirits, beers and soft drinks supply contract with a view to renegotiating our punitive clauses and to potentially introduce a new supplier. After several months of negotiation *CRC* secured a deal for us. Without their drive, momentum and expertise our new contract would never have been concluded. We now have a first class supplier and are not only achieving savings, but also a larger volume of business."

Umesh Umatt, Director

ROYAL UNITED HOSPITAL BATH

"I approached the water project with *The Cost Reduction Company* with a lot of scepticism as we thought we had already exhausted the opportunities to reduce water consumption. *The Cost Reduction Company* delivered precisely what they said they would; innovative technology, simple to maintain and delivering savings. I would encourage all *NHS Trusts* to conduct an analysis of their water usage for their site as we found it beneficial. In our particular circumstances we used *CRC* to good effect. This technology is saving us over £40,000 a year."

Andy House, Head of Estates, RUH Bath

STANFORD HALL

"On the edge of the estate I run a small caravan park. Its single largest expense, greater even than wages and salaries, is electricity. I asked *The Cost Reduction*

Company to investigate the account and was amazed to discover that we could save slightly more than 50% of historic annual costs, at prices fixed for the next two years in the face of increasing energy prices. This is a powerful shot in the arm and a morale boost for this particular small business. I have therefore asked the CRC to investigate other areas of expenditure over the whole estate."

Anthony Hughes-Onslow

CALDICOTT SCHOOL

"*The Cost Reduction Company* has now worked with Caldicott for three years. During this time they have been instrumental in making substantial savings to the school's overheads. Furthermore they have been, and still are, thinking of new ways to make savings… I am very happy to do business with a company where you only pay them if they make savings. It is a 'win-win' situation for all and as such I have no hesitation in recommending their services."

Adrian Hollyer, Bursar, Caldicott School

COX GREEN SCHOOL

"The reaction after we had secured a rebate on an academy's gas account, against all odds: 'Your under whelmed 'quite pleased' is in contrast to my amazed delight!! Thank you for all your work on this – it's great news.'"

Gill Newman, Business Manager
Cox Green School, Maidenhead

Contents

Preface

WHAT WE DO AT THE COST REDUCTION COMPANY

The idea behind cost reduction is a relatively simple one. The aim is to generate revenue without having to make additional sales, by drawing out benefits from elements that are already available to you – you just have to put in the work to find them!

The trouble is, most businesses don't have time to carry out the process by themselves.

It all boils down to one indisputable truth: reducing costs is a proactive strategy, not a reactive task! We found that most businesses already had their hands full dealing with more immediate issues than reducing costs. If your staff are under constant pressure to deliver their sales then 80%, 90%, maybe even 100% of their time will be spent worrying about when and where their next client will materialise and, quite understandably, not on keeping down costs.

We therefore set up *The Cost Reduction Company* (CRC) to help businesses and schools reduce their day-to-day running costs. Happily, this allows them to spend their time focusing on what they are good at - running their core business and developing future prospects.

The importance of incorporating the combination of tariff reduction and consumption reduction quickly became apparent to us. There weren't many – perhaps any – companies working simultaneously in both areas. They tended to concentrate solely on tariffs or the green renewables market, whereas we thought it best to target both together. Reducing costs can be green and by being green you can also reduce your costs. That's what we do: we bring the two together.

Over time we have fine-tuned this theory into a working praxis. Now CRC focuses on both the consumption side and the tariff side. The problem with tariffs is that any initial reduction in cost is only of value for the length of the contract negotiated – you are only as good as the contract! You can work really hard to get your prices down but after two years it is likely to increase again. However hard you work you will always be playing second fiddle to the market and inflation. The only true way to reduce costs in the long -term is by using less.

We also recognise that one of the key factors in reducing the cost base of a business is a human one. Human behaviour plays a major part in rising costs and therefore plays a key part in reducing them.

My background is in hospitality and leisure. In the 80s, these industries were booming, but by the 90s they started to struggle because of rapidly increasing overheads. The break-even point was forever rising; so we had to concentrate on reducing costs in all areas. It was through this focus I began honing the skills and practices that would one day become our approach at *The Cost Reduction Company.*

For me cost reduction isn't necessarily a science; it is more about common sense. What we do isn't rocket science! We spend a considerable amount of time researching the markets, finding the best suppliers and then carrying out the necessary due diligence.

The majority of books on the topic of cost reduction are swamped with jargon, which is completely unnecessary. Good, clear communication is an absolutely vital part of cost reduction.

My job is not to confuse you, but to help you reduce your costs. For me, our business starts and ends with using less. This is the simple message we aim to get across: *just use less!*

Why waste money if you can run a business for 15% less money and it doesn't affect the performance and quality of your services?

You can use these extra savings to drive the business forward. It gives you the choice to spend that 15% on whatever you want.

Over the years, we've had considerable success in the education sector. We've realised that if we can change the culture in schools, to use less, then we can make a real difference in the long-term. We have therefore, set up an education programme called **USING LESS!** that strives to spread the importance of our cost-saving ideas.

Currently *The Cost Reduction Company* works with in excess of 50 independent schools, 25 academies, 20 NHS Private Health sites and a range of institutions in the UK, including *Lord's Cricket Ground.*

Our many clients have been delighted to discover the joys of using less stuff, saving money and helping the planet … and you will too!

BEFORE YOU START

Here's a checklist of some of the most common costs that can be reduced. So you can get the most out of this book, take a few moments to tick (✔):

- I know how much I am currently spending in this area
- I have checked prices in the last six months
- I can save money in this area

Area of Cost	I know how much I am spending	I have checked prices in the last 6 months	I can save money in this area
Gas	❏	❏	❏
Electricity	❏	❏	❏
Oil	❏	❏	❏
Fuel	❏	❏	❏
Telephones	❏	❏	❏
Lighting	❏	❏	❏
Waste	❏	❏	❏
Water	❏	❏	❏
Stationery	❏	❏	❏
Textbooks	❏	❏	❏

Printing	❏	❏	❏
Photocopying	❏	❏	❏
Office supplies	❏	❏	❏
Cleaning	❏	❏	❏
Maintenance	❏	❏	❏
Vehicles	❏	❏	❏
Transport	❏	❏	❏
Raw materials	❏	❏	❏
IT/Internet	❏	❏	❏
Equipment	❏	❏	❏
Grounds maintenance	❏	❏	❏
Coaches	❏	❏	❏
Credit cards	❏	❏	❏
Accounting	❏	❏	❏
Finance costs	❏	❏	❏
Bank fees/charges	❏	❏	❏
Compliance	❏	❏	❏
Carbon Reduction Commitment	❏	❏	❏
Servicing	❏	❏	❏
Food	❏	❏	❏
Entertaining	❏	❏	❏
Other	❏	❏	❏

How did you do? Did you get any insights from this activity?

Chapter One

THE SIX MOST COMMON MISTAKES

Key questions:
How do you start to reduce your costs?
Where do most companies go wrong?

Here is a quick list of the six most common mistakes made when running organisations:

1. Not knowing exactly how much your company is spending.
2. Not knowing how much your company *should* be spending.
3. Not knowing exactly what you want to buy.
4. Not regularly measuring your usage.
5. Not taking action and not resourcing.
6. Not communicating clearly.

One of the key messages I hope to get across in this book is that **TIME**, or more specifically a lack of time, is a key obstruction to effective cost reduction. Finding and setting aside the time to work out the best way to reduce your costs is half the battle. So it's not my intention to take this time away from you with dense blocks of text. I am going to keep things simple. Hopefully, this list of the six most common mistakes will act as a helpful starting point.

MISTAKE 1

NOT KNOWING EXACTLY HOW MUCH YOUR COMPANY IS SPENDING

Do you know how much your business is spending on each category of cost? Well, if not then you need to act swiftly to acquire a breakdown of all your costs. You need to be on top of everything; you need to know:

- How much the company is spending on this!
- How much the company is spending on that!
- Which department is spending what, and on what!
- Which department is spending the most!
- Which department is spending the least!
- What the greatest cost is!

In any business it is highly beneficial, as well as extremely convenient, to measure the costs of each and every department separately. The thinking behind this is, by making individual departments fully responsible for their own costs, you are pinning responsibility directly on those who are spending the money and inflicting these costs upon the company. Implementing an overall strategy of measuring how much you spend by line is vital, as it allows you to fully understand the true spend in each area and to negotiate accordingly with your suppliers.

I often come across companies that seem happy to remain completely oblivious to how their cost structure is made up. This can cause all sorts of problems, as you need to know where your costs are coming from.

For instance, you could have a situation at a company where one department buys stationery and cleaning materials from one supplier and another buys stationery and print supplies from a different supplier. The second of these suppliers is charging the second department an inflated price for the stationery. They would get it much cheaper if they bought it from the first supplier; however, they, and you, are completely unaware of this opportunity to reduce costs because you have failed to produce a breakdown of expenditure to analyse. A full breakdown – *line by line* – is necessary to let you know exactly what you are spending and on what, as well as to indicate where changes can be made to reduce it.

Tip
Compare individual costs for last year and this year, and you might see some obvious savings.

MISTAKE 2

NOT KNOWING HOW MUCH YOUR COMPANY *SHOULD* BE SPENDING

It is one thing knowing exactly what your company is spending and another thing knowing if this amount is the correct amount to be spending.

First of all, what do I mean by the *correct* amount? I have heard many clients argue that it is subjective and claim that the amount they are spending is the right amount for their company for various short-sighted reasons. They might claim that they don't mind spending £35,000 on their annual electricity bill because they have always done so. A lot of businesses harbour a *"Because we always have!"* attitude. A company might also be happy with their high costs because they see them as being relatively cheap compared to some of their other costs.

Thinking like this is just lazy! Your company will suffer if you don't produce and regularly analyse a breakdown of your cost structure and actively seek out ways to reduce costs. The easiest way to do this is to compare your costs with the costs of similar-size companies or your competitors to see if your current spending is needlessly excessive.

This technique is called **BENCHMARKING**. It is an effective way of checking your current costs against what your costs should or could be.

Another effective way of reducing costs is to outsource the entire cost reduction process to an outside company to benefit from their specialised expertise. Allowing your company to be examined by a fresh set of eyes can benefit your company enormously, as the outside company's objective perspective will transcend the subjective gaze of you and your employees.

Subjectivity leads to familiarity, which in turn leads to comfort and indolence. An objective view can shake up and wake your company from its languorous slumber and enlighten you and your employees to new ways of reducing costs. A specialist company's experience in this field means their suggestions have been tried and tested.

Tip
Look for benchmarking opportunities and talk to local companies and suppliers to find out how much you should be spending.

MISTAKE 3

NOT KNOWING EXACTLY
WHAT YOU WANT TO BUY

If you don't take the time to thoroughly define your specification you will invite all sorts of trouble that can affect your pricing and ultimately your company's profit. Again, trouble is easy to avoid. All you have to do is take the time and effort to really think about what you want to buy and make sure this is taken into consideration and explicitly understood by all parties involved when the product is acquired.

Imagine that I have gone shopping because I need a new wallet.

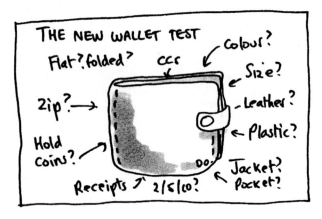

This may sound like a simple enough task, but there are a multitude of things to think about to ensure I come away with a wallet that satisfies my needs.

To list a few:

- What colour?
- What size?
- Should it be made of leather or plastic?
- Does it need credit card slots?
- Do I want it to fit in a pocket?
- Do I want it to last 2 years/ 5 years/ 10 years?
- Should it hold receipts?
- Does it need a pocket for change?
- Does it need a zip?
- Does it need to be flat or folding?

Now imagine that someone else is going to the shop to buy the wallet for me. They need to know the extent of my preferences – every single answer to this list of questions – otherwise they will return with the wrong wallet. It is a matter of good, clear communication.

So something that at first seems straightforward actually requires a fair amount of information. If you translate this to something more complex, for instance an extensive cleaning project of a large school, you can see the importance of knowing exactly what you want.

It is also important to distinguish between **CHEAP** and **VALUE.** There is a whole lot more to reducing costs than seeking out cheaper alternatives to your current pricing. Cheap goods are usually cheap for a reason. What you need is value!

Tip
Listen to the people using the service or product and write down what could be done to improve it.

MISTAKE 4

NOT REGULARLY MEASURING YOUR USAGE

Are you carefully, systematically and thoroughly monitoring your utility costs? If not, you may be falling prey to needless costs due to overconsumption. It is important to take a **SYSTEMATIC APPROACH** to measuring your consumption. If you do not read your meters and track your usage on a regular basis, it becomes almost impossible to counter excessive usage. For starters, if you are not completely on top of your usage, you will not be aware that you are wasting your resources in the first place.

Anyone involved in using electricity, gas, water or oil needs to know how much their individual usage is costing the company and then needs to be given a target to reduce it immediately if it is found to be excessive. It is usually possible to reduce utility usage by up to 20% by altering human behaviour, as human beings have a natural tendency to be wasteful.

Remember this includes all staff equally. Those at the top must be aware of their usage as much as everybody else.

Without a clear monitoring and measuring system it is impossible to gauge where resources are being wasted. Technology is the key. Computerised monitoring systems can be effective ways of recording employees' consumption, making them personally accountable.

The mismanagement of stationery is a classic example, as people often squirrel away stationery supplies just in case they run out. By implementing an efficient management system, like a computerised system with a next day delivery option, you can ensure a large reduction in stock as well as usage. It's really just an issue of ironing out bad habits!

Tip
Instigate a monthly report that tells you how much you spend and use compared with last month and last week.

MISTAKE 5

NOT TAKING ACTION
AND NOT RESOURCING

Your costs won't reduce themselves! You need to take action. You need to commit to the project and put in the required time and effort. A lot of companies fall at this first hurdle and never really get going!

As I see it, the main problem is that most businesses are focused on reactive processes, dealing with the here and now, the day-to-day. No one has the time to fully commit to the process of reducing costs because they instinctively prioritise and are preoccupied with the immediacy of reactive tasks.

For instance, just think about organising your family's summer holiday. This isn't a simple process; there's a lot to think about. You get home from work and, after dinner, begin your research by scrolling through holiday comparison websites and reading the mountain of holiday brochures that your family has accumulated since last year's holiday.

However, only five minutes in, you receive a phone call from a colleague saying there is a work-related issue that needs your immediate attention. The holiday is no longer the priority. You think, *"I can do that later; we're not going for another five months!"* The holiday brochures are brushed to one side as you revert to work mode. The planning of the holiday is already forgotten.

Cost reduction, much like holiday planning, is a proactive task, not a reactive task. Reactive tasks are prioritised because you simply cannot afford to ignore them at that precise moment. On the surface, proactive tasks do not demand such immediate attention, but if you are serious about reducing your costs you need to take action now otherwise you will never find the time. It will be too late!

The most effective way of dealing with these issues is to outsource the cost reduction process to an outside company. By doing this, you can happily focus on dealing with reactive tasks and running your core business. This approach allows you to **WORK SMART!**

If you would rather undertake the cost reduction programme in-house, you need to start straight away. The first step is to set up a committee and to elect a leader to chair the meetings and drive the cost reduction process forward.

Tip
Put an action plan in place with timings and targets. Make it easy at first so you can build on your initial success.

MISTAKE 6

NOT COMMUNICATING CLEARLY

Excellent communication is the key to cost reduction!

You need to be asking the right questions of the right people. The idea is to be in a position where you have all the relevant information necessary to make informed decisions on a wide array of issues, such as defining the specification, motivating your staff, dealing with your suppliers, measuring consumption, creating a cost reduction team, working out what your customers expect or working with an outside company.

BATMAN, THERE'S NO EASY WAY TO SAY THIS: YOU NEED TO INTRODUCE A CALL-OUT FEE

For these reasons, improving communication skills will help enormously in dealing with every single one of the five other common mistakes.

Therefore, don't be surprised to see the statement, *"Excellent communication is the key to cost reduction!"* crop up repeatedly throughout this book.

If you only take away one message, let it be that communication is absolutely essential to reducing costs.

Good communication skills are the most valuable when dealing with your own staff. This is particularly true when embarking on a cost reduction programme. You need to identify who is going to help reduce your costs and how they are going to do it. In truth, the whole company needs to be involved.

It is the job of the CEO to make sure that staff members are motivated and given the correct tools to reduce the company's costs. Motivation is ignited by giving everyone an opportunity to voice their ideas.

So how do you ensure your employees can have their say and feed their ideas through middle management to the board? It is not just the case that ideas need collating and analysing. The CEO needs to establish an environment where every single member of the company feels valued and free to voice their opinion. Ideas for reducing costs can come from any employee in any department!

Just as important as being open to ideas is rewarding these ideas. If an employee proposes an idea they need to be told why you have or haven't chosen to implement it. If an idea is successful, the employee who suggested it needs to be rewarded.

Tip
Implement a weekly update for all staff. It is important to do the simple things first to gain momentum.

Chapter Two

THE EFFECTS OF REDUCING COSTS CAN BE DRAMATIC

Key Questions
In what ways are the effects of cost reduction
dramatic? What will an increase in cash flow mean for
your business? What does it mean to shift from short to
long-term thinking? What does this mean for a charity?

IS IT WORTH IT?

I am occasionally asked outright whether cost reduction is worth it. There is a simple answer to this question.

Yes. Just take a look at Diagram 2.1!

Whenever I'm asked to present on this topic, I begin with this simple demonstration. It's a quick way to show that the effects of cost reduction can be really dramatic and significantly increase profits.

TURNOVER = £1M   PROFIT = £100,000

SAVING 5% ON COSTS OF £900,000 = £45,000

= 45% INCREASE IN PROFITS!

Diagram 2.1 Cost reductions and increased profits

Imagine that a company is reviewing its annual figures. For the year in question the company made an annual turnover of £1 million, which, after taking all its various costs into account, works out as £100,000 worth of profit.

The company wants to know what effect reducing their costs can have on their profit for the next year. They will implement a cost reduction programme that should save them a modest 5% on their costs. This 5% saving is equivalent to £45,000, as this is 5% of their £900,000 worth of costs. As their profits were only £100,000, this equates to a massive 45% increase in profits.

At first, this seems rather surprising. I find that people are often taken aback. But it's simple mathematics. The effects of reducing your costs will be dramatic! So, in short, the answer to the question, *'Is it worth the effort?'* is an unequivocal YES!

Reducing cost allows several things to happen. The most fundamental effect is a cash flow improvement in the business, but once these savings are made there are lots of ways to use this extra money.

One real benefit is that cost reduction allows you to relax. In a relaxed working environment you can think about the future, work creatively and your staff can carry on with their work knowing their jobs are safe. You should keep reminding your employees that if the company is successful in reducing costs it will increase profits leading to the expansion of the company, which, amongst other things, will mean job security and perks for them.

This chapter will focus on the advantages of:

1. Keeping your core business intact
2. Shifting from short-term to long-term thinking
3. Reducing the need for overdraft
4. Rewarding your staff

KEEPING YOUR CORE BUSINESS INTACT

A successful cost reduction programme will allow you to make significant savings without having to disrupt your core business, which is the last thing you want to do. You want to maintain a steady ship! You will not be able to enjoy the advantages of reducing your costs if you have achieved savings by disrupting your core business. Staff redundancies can be a quick way to reduce costs, but you need to think about the serious repercussions.

First, sacking staff will breed a general feeling of discontent and poor morale in the office. Second, you have employed your staff to perform particular tasks. Unless the work they are doing is completely unnecessary, you will be left with a large hole to fill.

It is all good reducing costs, but if you mess around with your core business you won't have the resources to function efficiently and your revenue will diminish. Your core business must remain intact!

If you manage to reduce costs without affecting your core business then your staff will enjoy the advantages of cost reduction. With the increase in cash flow you will reduce the need to lay off staff. Tell your staff that if the company reduces costs substantially then you will use these savings to guarantee their jobs are safe. This is not only a great motivation in itself, but also lets your staff know that you appreciate their role as part of the core business and that the last thing you want is to let them go. Your employees can then knuckle down to work without fearing the next redundancy.

Happy employees are loyal and more productive.

If people know that their jobs are safe for the long term, that their work is truly appreciated and that their role is invaluable to the company then they are more likely to be fully focused on doing their best to help move the business forward. Make sure this motivation gets through to them!

"You won't be able to enjoy the advantages of reducing your costs if you gained them by disrupting your core business!"

THE SHIFT FROM SHORT-TERM TO LONG-TERM THINKING

An improvement in cash flow allows you to relax as you no longer have to worry about the immediacy of financial burdens. This allows you to start thinking creatively about the future and switch from short-term to long-term goals. Your time is not absorbed with problem solving. Instead, you have the time and money to invest in the future and strategise.

Businesses are generally focused on reactive tasks. These are emergencies that need to be sorted out **NOW!** Companies often get bogged down in the day-to-day reality of dealing with problems that require immediate attention with no opportunity to think about what lies beyond the horizon. By reducing your costs, and freeing up cash flow within your company, you will find yourself with the opportunity to break free from this reactive dirge and can start thinking creatively about exploring whole new worlds of possibility.

For starters, you can allocate funds for exciting new projects that expand the core business. You can also look to invest in marketing to improve sales and work on new marketing initiatives to improve the company brand.

You could also turn your gaze toward the future by investing in technology. For instance, reducing utility costs by 3-5% may allow you to invest in new technology to reduce long-term consumption. As utility prices are continually increasing, this saving is compounded each year by the increase in utility prices, allowing you to save more and more as the value price keeps soaring.

Your staff will feel like they are part of something interesting and dynamic if they can see that money is being invested in moving the company forward. Your staff will think: *"This isn't just another office job; I am part of an innovative company that is going somewhere!"* This will encourage them to work even harder and take greater pride in their work.

Creative growth will allow you to retain your best and brightest and most ambitious personnel, who might otherwise be tempted to move on. Similarly, you will be able to attract higher calibre employees in the future to your flourishing company or organisation.

Of course, the same can be said for clients. If you make substantial investment in the company – whether in marketing to improve the brand, in technology to improve productivity or in training to improve customer service – the expansion of your company will be there for all to see. It will be apparent to potential clients that your company is thriving and healthy.

All in all, an improvement in cash flow enables you to switch from stressful day-to-day short-term thinking to relaxed and creative long-term thinking. When you relax the business moves forward, and it allows you to take risks and make investments for the future. Once the savings are made there are many ways to use this money. A wise investment creates a snowball effect, taking your company up, up and away from your market competitors.

REDUCING THE NEED FOR OVERDRAFT

If your company is in poor shape you could find yourself spending more time in the bank than in the office. There is nothing as stressful as being at the mercy of your bank manager and nothing as horrifying as that suffocating feeling that you and your organisation are slowly being swallowed up by the bank's ever increasing interest rates. It is a sinking sensation, a bit like quick sand except that it's not you sinking into the ground but your company's money sinking further and further into the banker's pocket! A cash flow improvement will reduce the need for overdraft facilities and therefore the amount of time you spend in the bank nervously asking for loans.

A cash flow improvement will set you free.

There are two advantages to this. First, you can enjoy the immediate cost saving of the interest you no longer have to pay. This money can now be put to more productive use, rather than just straight into the banker's pocket.

But this isn't the only advantage. You can also forget the stress of worrying about overdraft payments and meetings with the bank manager. You should think about this in terms of opportunity cost. You are now free to focus on other tasks. This not only gives you more time to focus on your core business, but allows you to relax, become creative and drive new initiatives.

REWARD YOUR STAFF

Initially when embarking on reducing costs the morale in a company can be low, as staff members fear redundancies. If you can reduce costs without axing staff, the process motivates your staff to chase the best savings and search for opportunities to improve the company.

There are many ways to reward your staff, which may not have been possible before you had reduced your costs and freed up cash flow. You can offer your staff a whole range of rewards for their hard work. It could be a holiday, a weekend away, a dinner with the CEO, a monetary bonus, a bottle of champagne, a lavish box of chocolates, or it could simply be recognition among their peers with a wall plaque, trophy, or speeches of thanks in front of colleagues and their families at a social function.

You might have an employee who has been a key part of your organisation for the last five years. This person has been exceptionally consistent with their hard working approach, always being the first one in and last one out, but, due to a lack of funds, you could not afford to offer a promotion. Well, now you have the funds to do so.

The important thing is your employees feel their hard work and long hours are being appreciated. The key is to let them know they are valued and appreciated. All you need to do is tell them!

Don't be afraid to communicate!

"An increase in cash flow allows you to relax as you no longer have to worry about the immediacy of financial burdens!"

With the money generated from cost reduction you could introduce a high-tech feedback or reward system so it's easier to reward your staff. As well as champagne, weekends away and the monetary bonuses, you could allocate more of your time to personally letting your staff know they are doing a great job. This will have a positive effect on the office, increasing morale and improving your relationship with members of your teams.

Always keep in mind that a happy office is more likely to be a productive office. It is also nice to see that your employees are working with a smile on their faces.

Your employees may even look forward to going to work in the morning!

RELEASE CASH FROM STOCK

By scrutinising consumption, you can check stock levels and efficiencies that allow you to release cash sitting in your stores or company offices. These savings have always been there. Only by going through the cost reduction process did you became aware and see the opportunity to release the money from stagnation. Now your company can benefit from this increase in cash flow.

THE BENEFITS FOR A CHARITY

If you reduce operating costs you will increase the amount of money going directly into your charity, allowing cash to reach its goals.

This gives you a story to tell your supporters and should result in increased donations. In general, people are concerned when giving to charity that only a small proportion of their donation is actually reaching those in need. If you reduce your costs you can use the improved cash flow to make sure that the money reaches its target, and then let people know about it! Highlight this in your advertising campaigns! You will see a great spike in donations.

Would you rather donate to a charity that says 75% of all the money donated goes directly to those in need or to a rival charity that only gives 50% to the needy?

This principle applies to schools and universities too. You could write to your pupils and their parents saying: *"Owing to our effective cost saving activity, we are reducing our fees next year by 5%!"*

What an inspiring story!

How surprised and grateful would parents be to receive a drop in fees, instead of the usual hike in fees?

You can use the same method to attract potential pupils by ensuring parents their children will directly benefit from your school's cost saving activity if they enrol. You could write in the school's prospectus that, *"Owing to our effective cost saving activity, we will strive to keep fees reasonably priced, whilst we endeavour to improve facilities, so that your children will get the best education possible, beginning with a new IT lab from September!"*

Parents will prefer to send their children to a school with a new IT lab than to one with outdated equipment. Reducing your costs can really help to sell your school and attract new students, as long as you can show you are using savings to invest in quality education.

CHAPTER SUMMARY

- *The most immediate effect of reducing costs is a cash flow improvement*

- *Use savings to keep your core business intact*

- *Increase staff morale by reducing the fear of redundancy*

- *Make the change from short-term to long-term thinking*

- *Reduce the need for an overdraft*

- *Reward your staff*

- *Look out for cash wasting away in stocks*

- *Charities can now provide more revenue for their causes*

Chapter Three

USING LESS STUFF!

Key questions:
What is 'Using Less'? Why is it relevant to you?
How should you go about reducing consumption?

INFORMATION AND EDUCATION

This chapter is about consumption reduction and how working toward achieving sustainability and being more *green* can hugely benefit your business or school. I shall look at the rewards of reducing your company's consumption, describe why these will be long-lasting and discuss the practical means by which they can be achieved.

First, I will outline the main characteristics of *The Cost Reduction Company's* new initiative called *Using Less*, which focuses on working within the education sector to reduce costs through consumption reduction while simultaneously providing an educational package for children and staff. This approach can also be used in business and office environments.

The principle of **USING LESS** is about educating for **SOCIAL RESPONSIBILITY**. The key to education is learning and measuring improvement. We want our kids and our staff to understand the benefits of taking our surroundings and community into account when making decisions about how we live our lives and how we treat our resources. When we make decisions regarding purchasing in our day-to-day lives, we need to understand why we need the product and what the effect will be if we don't have it.

Regardless of whether you are a Headmaster or a CEO, this is an important subject. You need to know why *Using Less* is important to you!

WHY IS USING LESS RELEVANT TO ME?

Venturing into the field of environmental impact, you need to keep in mind the way the world is today – the whole doom and gloom side of things – which is effectively a population explosion and the fact that we are running out of resources. We don't know exactly what state the world will be in 15 or 20 years from now but all indicators point to a scenario where we are putting serious pressure on feeding the world's population. This could mean famine, global instability and even war.

The problem in most organisations is that there is a lone wolf howling in the dark about the looming global crisis but nobody else is taking a blind bit of notice. The environmental experts have been shouting for the rest of us to change our consumption habits for several years.

The collective apathy is like the health warnings on cigarette packets telling smokers they are severely increasing their risk of lung cancer and other diseases. They just shrug and say, *"Okay"* and light up another cigarette. The bigger global picture is not necessarily what matters to most of us, mainly because we can't see the personal relevance in the here and now.

However, no one can deny the simple truth that the human population is increasing and resources are finite.

So what the issue comes down to is: **"WHY IS IT RELEVANT TO ME?"** It's such a big challenge; we must try to comprehend what being more sustainable, being more 'green', *Using Less*, means for us and our particular school or business. The angle I want to push is that it is relevant to us all on a financial level.

It will save you money!

For instance, let's take a look at utilities. In terms of *Using Less*, the glittering prize lies with utilities because this is where the big money will be saved.

It is inevitable that the price of oil and gas and other energy resources will continue to rise simply because resources will be scarcer, harder to come by and therefore more expensive.

Look at the graph in Diagram 3.1 on page 46. At the moment households, schools and businesses alike, are increasing general expenditure in line with line *A,* in accordance with the *Retail Price Index.*

However, because of the inevitable inflation on the price of oil, electricity and gas, what actually happens to utility expenditure is more in the region of *B*.

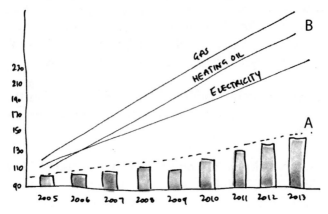

Diagram 3.1 Retail Price Index - All Items Nb/ Index 2005 = 100

A huge gulf is emerging between how much we *expect to pay* for utilities at our current levels of consumption and how much we *will be* charged. This gap will continue to widen as we move into the future, spiralling out of control for many businesses. Likewise, if we act now to reduce our consumption, the saving increases as the years go by.

The message is clear!

Over the next five years we must reduce our usage by 10%, 15%, maybe 20%. The effect of bringing down consumption today will have huge benefits further along the line. This is why it should be seen as an urgent priority.

So the question then becomes: *What am I prepared to pay to get that reduction down?*

As is often the case, people will argue that they have more important and immediate issues at hand. The question I ask of those who postpone using less energy is: *"How can you afford not to do this?"*

Since 2007, the government has been stepping up its initiatives and policies aimed at reducing carbon emissions, setting an ambitious target of an 80% reduction by 2050. An important part of this is the *Carbon Reduction Commitment Scheme*, also known as the *CRC Energy Efficiency Scheme*, which targets large organisations such as supermarkets, banks and government departments. Organisations will qualify for the scheme based on their electricity usage.

Although this was initially only aimed at larger organisations, it won't stay that way for long. Phase 2 and Phase 3 of this legislation will target smaller organisations and kicks in soon. In particular, any organisation that operates 24/7 will be looked at and will need to reduce their usage. Therefore, schools will soon be involved. It means you cannot afford to not start Using Less, as you will receive penalty fines from the government if you don't!

As well as this, costs associated with waste disposal are becoming more expensive, especially food waste. Composting is now essential due to large increases in landfill tax. Not to mention the costs arising from the disposal of electrical items etc.

We want our clients to spend their money on what they choose, not on costs they are needlessly amassing because of spiralling utility costs. Let's reduce consumption so we can buy goods that will improve life. For schools, this could mean a new mini bus, the latest equipment for the hockey team or new computers for the ICT lab.

Using Less will help you use fewer resources and save lots of money! If we can agree on this principle, then we need to educate the next generation, which is why CRC has targeted the education sector.

"Using Less will save money for your school or business!"

THE MONITORING SYSTEM

Where to begin? Only once you know what you are **USING NOW**, can you start **USING LESS.**

The key is information. It is your duty to know if you are using excess resources. You need to know *what* is happening *now!* You need to know *how much* you are using *now!* You need to know *who* is using what *now!* If you have this information, you can fix these problems. You can work to ensure your organisation is more resourceful now and in the future.

The starting point is knowing where you are right now!

That is, how much electricity do you use in each building? Which building is the most inefficient? And the least? Which department, classroom, boarding house? How much oil, gas and water are you actually using? How much paper, textbooks, stationery, food, cleaning supplies, sports equipment?

Utilities should be number one priority – as this is where the big savings are – but there are significant savings to be made in small items too. For instance, a simple way of keeping track of food wastage is to collect all wasted food in a rubbish bin at the end of lunch and weigh it. That tells you how much food is being wasted.

All this information allows us to draw a line under where you are now. From there we can begin an analysis of the results, which will allow us to identify an action plan. It will also help us recognise where to find quick wins.

But, how are we supposed to record all this information?

One of our tag lines at *The Cost Reduction Company* is: **SAVINGS THROUGH INNOVATION**. What's needed is cutting edge technology. As part of the *Using Less* initiative, we provide a **computerised monitoring system** which is easy to install and allows you to see exactly what's going on with utility usage in real time.

This system is set up in our head office at *The Cost Reduction Company*. It allows us to review our usage in terms of cost, carbon and power etc. At any moment I can quickly switch to a live feed to assess what's happening right now as well as check what's been happening throughout the night.

Early in the morning before the rest of the staff arrive, there is little power being used. However, I can see spikes of activity throughout the night, every few hours or so. Obviously, no one should be in the office at three in the morning. This information gives me the opportunity to ask, *"What has been going on?"* I can speak to the maintenance man. The chances are that someone has left a heater on overnight. The new technology provides an opportunity to investigate so I can make sure it won't happen again.

At one boarding school, as soon as we started monitoring, we noticed that they were using as much electricity in the boarding house during the day, when the boys were in classes, as they were in the early evening, when they were back in their dorms. A quick inspection showed that the boys were leaving their laptops and phone chargers plugged in throughout the day. All the school had to do was make sure this didn't continue and they would immediately reduce their electricity cost.

Teachers can actually use this monitoring technology in their classrooms. They can sit there with their pupils, project it up onto the whiteboard and explain what is going on with energy usage throughout the school.

The system's readings might indicate that the gym is currently using more heating than any other building. This might be because Year Three is about to have its PE lesson, soon to be followed by Years Five and Six. Although, it could be a day when there are no PE lessons scheduled. If this is the case then the gym doesn't need to be heated.

The entire school needs to be focused on the project. This means getting everybody involved: the head, the bursars, the teachers, the non-teaching staff, parents and children. You could have the monitoring system on display at assembly, in the reception area, on the school website and as part of the intranet.

Once we have the information, the next step is setting a target to achieve.

Define what counts as a success. The goal will be different for every school and organisation, but could be something like, *"A 10 % reduction in our electricity use by the end of the year."*

After agreeing on a target we must outline the ways we plan to achieve this. Steps can range from the complex to something as simple as ensuring all the lights are switched off at the end of the day.

It is also important to make sure we track our achievements, and recognise how well or how poorly we are doing. Both are equally important! So we must check the readings not monthly but weekly, perhaps even on a daily basis!

ACTION!

Plans, thoughts, ideas and goals are all very well, but the only thing that will make you reduce your costs is **TAKING ACTION!**

The danger when talking about sustainability is that it becomes more of a campaign than something rooted in practical actions.

This is where our initiative, *Using Less*, is of a different breed. It is about practical steps as opposed to getting swamped by doom and gloom.

So how do we do it?

A team from *The Cost Reduction Company* will visit once a term and present to the school or eco-committee, and set targets to achieve over the next year. We then talk about how we are going to achieve these targets. This is an on-going project set over two years. Someone needs to sit down every term and ask again: *"What are our targets?"*

We need to get buy-in from everyone involved in the school. So, who does this include? Who are the main stakeholders? The governors, the head, the bursar, the teachers, the non-teaching staff, the children and the parents. We need to make sure we communicate our message to everybody.

This isn't as easy as it might first seem. Perhaps, the obvious option would be to hold an assembly where we tell the children all about it. But in doing that, you don't get the governors, the bursar, the parents or any non-teaching staff.

Finding ways to communicate with the parents is important. First of all, you can communicate through the children. Encourage them to share what they have learnt; for instance, making sure their parents are recycling and all the lights are switched off at night. You can also reach the parents through the school website, where you can embed the monitoring system. There are also opportunities in the school newsletters, at parents' groups and on parents' evenings.

When it comes to the maintenance staff, we need to make sure that the relevant issues are addressed at their meetings. *Why are we doing that? Why are we doing this? What can we do to improve? What can we do to reduce our consumption?* They need to be constantly questioning why they are doing things and determining if there is anything they can do without.

At Half Term the maintenance man has to patrol the whole school remembering to manually switch off everything. I've had the experience of walking around on the first day of a new term and discovering a massive gym fully heated. I asked the maintenance man, *"What happened here?"* He said he was about to turn off the radiators when his phone started ringing and he must have forgotten to come back to finish the job.

Human nature means that mistakes will always be made. This is why it is important to establish a system that picks up when these errors have occurred. If you have a monitoring system, you will know if the heating has been left on and someone can quite easily go and turn it off.

It is important that the whole school community has strong motivation to get involved. A good way for a Headmaster to stir up motivation is to redefine savings in terms of what the school could purchase and really benefit from.

Let's imagine a school that has an unbeaten rugby team. Every week they journey across the county and never disappoint on the pitch. The only thing that lets them down is they turn up to away games in a crumbling, rusted shell of a minibus that has barely passed its MOT. It is universally agreed that the school needs to invest in a new one. Unfortunately, there are no funds.

COST SAVING IDEAS = RESOURCES WE NEED

How about saying, *"The plan is to reduce the school's consumption so we can buy a new mini bus!"* We have to say how much a new mini bus will cost. Let's say £50,000. We need to show visually how we are going about saving that exact sum of money. Every time we save another £10,000, we can mark it up on the board so that everyone can see that we are making real progress.

The responsibility has to be taken on by the school.

They need someone to help manage the project, which is where *The Cost Reduction Company* comes in, but the main brunt of the responsibility has to be embraced by the school. It is a commitment, but a necessary one because, at the end of the day, you will have more money available for the benefit of the students. The buy-in has to be: *we will save money!*

If everyone understands this then there is a real incentive and motivation to make progress.

Other ideas include organising an *Eco-Week* or *Green Week* as a catalyst to get the project going. And there is always an opportunity to seek out sponsorship from local companies interested in the potential client base the link with your school might bring. You could ask for sponsorship for an energy saving initiative at the school, such as an *Energy Cup*. This could be a competition where each department or boarding house goes head to head to see who can reduce their consumption the most.

MAKE USE OF YOUR STAFF

It's essential to encourage enthusiastic ideas from the staff because they are the ones who typi-cally know what is going on and who will have informed ideas about how to reduce usage. It could be the cleaner, the cook, the gardener or the office worker. These people have often been working for the school for many years and play an important role in the daily running and care of the premises.

I visited a school recently where they were complain-ing of a problem with the delivery of oil because in the winter the delivery truck had a tendency to get stuck in the snow. The previous year the tanker couldn't make it up the school drive, and they feared running out of oil. It was a boarding school, so this would have caused considerable hardship.

They decided to shut down the swimming pool and divert the oil from the swimming pool tank to the main school tank. The problem was solved creatively and everything was fine.

I had to ask the staff member, *"What did you do after the snow had gone?"* He said, *"Nothing, the guy still couldn't deliver the oil"* Our conversation continued: *"So you didn't actually interfere at all in the school's swimming schedule?" "That's right; no one was planning on using the pool!" "Well, why don't you carry on closing the swimming pool during those times so that you can continue using less oil?"*

The idea hadn't crossed his mind. He simply wasn't used to looking for opportunities to use less. If you can get the staff thinking about it, you will start heading in the right direction.

The Head is responsible for making sure everyone's ideas are heard.

At one school, when I spoke to the catering managers, I discovered they were frustrated about how much food was being wasted in their canteen every single day. They explained the children were only designated 15 minutes for lunch and would consequently pile up their plates, knowing they wouldn't have the time to go for seconds.

The problem was they could never finish all the food on their plates. The catering staff suggested that if the children were given an extra 15 minutes to eat their lunch they would be more prudent with the amount they chose. They estimated that food wastage would drop by around 20% as a result of this extension of the lunch break.

This on-going problem became entrenched due to lack of communication. The caterers were aware of what was going on and had come up with a solution, but had not been given the opportunity to tell someone in a position to sort it out. It was the fault of the school as an organisation that this had been allowed to continue. The school was needlessly throwing away money by wasting all this food.

More often than not, over-consumption arises from not listening to the people closest to the scene. And the problem can be avoided or solved by open two-way communication.

ADVICE FOR BUSINESSES

Just as in the education sector, the same principles apply for businesses. Saving money through *Using Less* relies on information and education.

Most of the time people are unaware of wasting resources. When an employee leaves his computer on overnight he is not considering the monetary impact this negligence is having on the company. He is either doing it by accident, out of habit or for the convenience of not waiting for it to power up each morning. This ignorance, however unintentional, is costing your company money and it's always worth doing something about wastage.

The chances are you only need to tell your staff once, and they will never do it again. This will certainly be the case with the small things, like forgetting to turn off the lights when leaving the office. So many people do this inadvertently, without thinking about it. At the end of the day your employees are more likely to be thinking about getting home to their families than whether they are the last one out and need to switch off the lights.

All that is needed is a poster on the wall saying: *"Will the last person out, please turn the lights off?"* If you don't remind them or show them how much it is costing the company, they won't change their attitude or habits.

Don't be afraid to provide education. How about involving all of your staff in a **GREEN DAY,** where they can learn all about the cost of leaving on the lights and other common energy inefficiencies.

If you let your employees know that their behaviour, however unintentional, is having a negative effect on the company, they will happily alter their behaviour. If it is clear to everyone that the company is making a considerable effort to stamp out needless waste of resources, they will also alter their behaviour. What is needed is a culture of **ACCOUNTABILITY.**

If your employees know they will be held accountable for their own personal consumption, they will jump at the chance to change their behaviour.

"What we are looking at here is changing human behaviour to alter your company's consumption!"

Bosses need to hold the main offenders accountable for their actions and bad habits. What we are looking at here is changing human behaviour to alter your company's consumption.

So, how should this be done? Again, it is all about information and communication. It is a process of finding out what is going on. Ask: *How much of our resources are being wasted? What kinds of resources tend to be wasted? Who is responsible for this wastage? What can we do to stop it?* By introducing a monitoring system that can record the consumption of your employees, you can quickly answer these questions and begin to reduce your costs.

The purpose of doing this is to create greater transparency in what resources are being used and by whom, so that you can maintain control of your usage and stock intake. This will curb consumption by making people accountable for their individual consumption. When people know that their bad habits are being monitored they will alter their behaviour. Basically, you are keeping tabs on your employees' actions so you can work out how best to reduce their consumption.

For instance, you can introduce a system where every-thing that an employee or department orders will now be recorded and billed showing who is responsible for what. Each member of staff is made to log in to an online system whenever they wish to order more stationery, for example. The process of ordering a new stapler consists in them finding their name on the PC's database so that they log in to their own account before they can order anything. This order is then recorded under their name and they are held accountable for the order and the item.

Their consumption is then measured and analysed on a monthly basis so that the right kinds of questions can be asked: *"Do you need to order so much?"* *"How come you ordered more or less than anyone else?"* *"Did you really need to order that extra stapler and all those paperclips?"* Human nature will kick in and people will quickly become aware of their bad habits. They will begin to work far more economically. Almost immediately, you will see a reduction in usage of around 10% to 20%.

This technology is used widely in shops and bars so that owners can keep track of how much their staff have been selling, as well as the particular items they have sold.

Let's take another example from the education sector. At the beginning of term, it is the responsibility of teachers to order text books for the coming year. If they need to order new ones, all they have to do is walk to the stationery shop and put in an order for the extra number they need. At the end of the year, when the stationery shop is asked who bought which books and who spent money on what, they have no idea as this information hasn't been recorded.

However, what if next term each teacher is asked to order their books using an online system, which instantly records what they have ordered including how many copies. When this information is reviewed at the end of the year, the school is alerted to the fact that there is a significant difference in the number of text books ordered by two teachers who teach the same subject. Mr Jones has ordered 35 text books, while Mr Smith has only ordered 25. The Head will be able to ask: *"Why?"* How were the extra books used?

Now that the information is available, the school can begin to do something about it. The school needs to find out why Mr Jones has ordered so many books and make sure he doesn't do so again.

Of course, it is important to be fair when making these kinds of judgments about who is in the wrong. At first, Mr Jones looks culpable simply because he has ordered so many books, but from this information alone you cannot possibly know the whole story.

This amount may have been necessary. Perhaps, his teaching methods are more thorough, and his students get better results because of this. Perhaps, Mr Smith has not ordered enough text books and is making some of his students share.

This information is the first step on the road to reducing your consumption, reducing costs and making profits. As long as you use this information correctly, ask the right questions and make a fair evaluation of the situation, you can begin to make progress.

Another way to reduce consumption is to adopt a more diligent approach to handling your delivery methods.

For instance, at schools, teachers will order large quantities of stationery at the beginning of the year, most of which will never be used. This stationery is often squirrelled away into the back of storage cupboards. I have heard of cases where schools have had to send back up to £20,000 of stock to its stationery supplier at the end of the year.

Now, if there was next day delivery, teachers could purchase the stationery only when they need it. If a teacher knows that she will be teaching a maths class requiring protractors, she can check her storage cupboard a day or two before to see if there are enough for all her pupils. If it so happens that she is a handful short then these protractors can be ordered straightaway. Again, it's all just a case of changing human behaviour to alter consumption. If this method is available to teachers, then they won't feel the need to order unnecessary stock and will take more care.

MAKING LARGE SAVINGS ON INVOICES

If you can reduce your consumption, you will receive benefits in all sorts of different places. I will demonstrate this with another example, one from the accounts department. Imagine your company is talking to a new supplier to provide you with all your stationery and cleaning materials. Instead of ordering from 20 different suppliers you have consolidated it under one.

The advantage of this is that you are now processing something like 12-24 invoices per year, instead of the previous total of maybe 600!

At a price of £35 per invoice processing, a price which is conservative according to the *Institute of Accountants*, you will be reducing the costs of your accounts department by a staggering £21,980 per annum. This sum could be seen as the equivalent of employing one whole person, who could technically be employed permanently as this total will now be saved each year.

As well as saving this large sum of £21,980, you will also benefit from the greater efficiency of having to read through less invoices. Before you consolidated all your orders through this new supplier, your accounts department had 600 invoices to check through. With such a large amount of invoices to inspect and review, human error is inevitable.

However hard working and skilled your accounts team, they are bound to make mistakes. By reducing the number of invoices to 24, they will be able to check them far more thoroughly and it will make for more efficient filing. Indeed, the 24 invoices are going to be much longer, as they still need to contain all the relevant content and detail, but with everything in one place your staff will find it easier to process.

THE LONG TERM EFFECT ON COST REDUCTION

The amount you pay for utilities will be an essential part of a company's cost structure. The positive effects of reducing your consumption of utilities will be dramatic and immediate and will last long into the future as well. If you reduce consumption by 10%, that saving is forever.

To illustrate what I mean by this, here's an example.

Your company is spending £100,000 per year on electricity. By introducing a cost reduction programme and paying particular attention to consumption, you reduce that by £10,000. Now, this £10,000 will not just be a one-off saving. Every time you receive your annual or biannual electricity bill the changes you have made ensure you of this 10% reduction of the bill, regardless of how much it has increased that year.

The measures you put in place to reduce consumption remain, as do their effects on your bill.

Now, electricity tariffs increase, year by year. So, in one years' time, when you renegotiate the price with your electricity provider the chances are that it will now be costing you something like 10% more as the prices have gone up.

You could look at this and say to yourself that you are now back at square one because you can offset this extra increase with the savings you made over the year.

However, there is more to it than this. The changes you made ensure that the 10% savings will last forever.

On top of this, the savings you make will increase in relation to the increase in price.

Imagine that your electricity bill rises as shown in Diagram 3.2.

Electricity costs

Year 1 = £100,000
Year 2 = £110,000
Year 3 = £121,000

Diagram 3.2 Electricity costs

So, in the first year it costs £100,000. In the second year this rises to £110,000. In the third year this rises even further to £121,000.

Now that you have put in the measures to reduce your consumption by 10%, you will always continue to save this 10% equivalent each and every year that follows. The amount you save is dependent on how sharply the utility price rises. The more it rises the more you will save. This is illustrated in Diagram 3.3.

Reduced consumption by 10%

Year 1 = £10,000
Year 2 = £11,000
Year 3 = £12,100

Diagram 3.2 Reduced consumption

In the first year this amounts to £10,000 (10% of £100,000), in the second year to £11,000 (10% of £110,000) and in the third year to £12,100 (10% of 121,000).

Remember, you can always use the funds saved to invest in even more utility reducing technology.

CHAPTER SUMMARY

• *Excellent communication is a must*

• *The key is information*

• *Know what you are **USING NOW** to begin **USING LESS***

• *Using Less will save you money*

• *Find out what is being wasted and how*

• *Find out who is responsible and make them accountable*

• *Alter your consumption by ironing out bad habits*

• *Results will be long lasting and dramatic*

Chapter Four

OUTSOURCING

Key questions:
What is outsourcing? What can you hope to gain by
allowing an objective view? Wouldn't it be cheaper and
easier to do it yourself? What is benchmarking?

OBJECTIVITY AND TIME

There are two major advantages in turning to outside help when your company is looking to reduce costs. The first is introducing an **OBJECTIVE VIEW** and the second is **SAVING TIME.**

An objective perspective can be invaluable in shaking up the deep-rooted traditions that are sure to lie hidden from the subjective gaze with which you view your own company. As well as this, it will provide a rigorous challenge to any preconceived ideas of how you believe your business should be run.

Of course, I am not talking about a bunch of mysterious strangers coming in and introducing all kinds of weird and wonderful business strategies and bizarre, revolutionary innovations. I am talking about the huge benefit of something that is actually rather simple.

What I want to highlight is the benefit of another viewpoint, which is distanced from the custom and comfort of your current business practice. It is normal to be fixated on the day-to-day running of your business, meaning that you will most likely be too involved in the small details to see the larger picture. This is only natural. Remember that human beings are, by nature, creatures of habit.

There are four main benefits in adopting the objective view of an outside company. These are:

1. Asking difficult questions
2. Cutting through the (office) politics
3. Benchmarking
4. Relevant expertise

"The most common reason that companies don't focus on reducing their costs is that they simply can't find the time!"

Bringing in an outside company will also buy you time, something which is perhaps even more valuable. Time is a precious thing. To revert to the usual cliché - time is money. Let's not forget that all business is geared toward making money. In business, by buying time, you are making profits.

The most common reason that a lot of companies don't focus enough on reducing their costs is that they simply can't find the time. Perhaps it is more accurate to say that they can't afford to spend the time doing it themselves.

Most businesses will want to utilise their resources to deal with more immediate problems; problems that need to be looked at and solved today. Their staff is only employed for a set amount of hours per day and they must occupy themselves with dealing with more immediate tasks aimed at fulfilling short-term goals and objectives. They do not have the time to be concerned with long-term cost reducing objectives. By outsourcing the task of reducing your costs, you can concentrate on running your core business, something I like to call **WORKING SMART!**

AN OUTSIDER CAN ASK DIFFICULT QUESTIONS

I want to begin with a story about an owner of a garden centre, who brought in an outside company to reduce his costs. For the sake of illustration and anonymity I shall call the owner Mr Perkins, and the garden centre, simply, *The Garden Centre*.

When looking at the cost base of *The Garden Centre*, the first thing which stood out was the high price that Mr Perkins was paying for his grass seed, an integral part of his business. He was, in fact, spending a total of £100,000 a year on grass seed. Of course, this expenditure stood out as excessive and was prioritised by the outside company as the first and most important thing to deal with.

When telling Mr Perkins that it was imperative they contact the supplier to negotiate a new deal, he was less than enthusiastic. His reason was the supplier was an old friend who had been supplying him with grass seed for near on 20 years. As well as this, he said that, once a year in the summer, the supplier would take him to the South of France to stay for a week in his luxury villa as part of the deal. In truth, it all boiled down to the reluctance of Mr Perkins to challenge the set price due to his concern he would upset his friend. This is where the view of an objective outsider is essential.

After much deliberation with Mr Perkins, the outside company contacted the supplier and said something along the lines of: *"We are here on behalf of Mr Perkins, who we understand is a good friend of yours. Unfortunately, he is in some financial trouble and really needs to reduce his costs. His biggest expenditure is the grass seed he orders from you and it would help him out enormously if we could reduce the price or arrange a discounted price."* Mr Perkins was afraid to put pressure on his friend with this up-front approach. However, the straight talking proved successful.

The supplier said that it would be his pleasure to help out Mr Perkins by offering a massive discounted price of 20%. Now, without being too cynical, it seems that what Mr Perkins considered a *friendship* was not necessarily reciprocated.

In fact, the grass seed supplier had probably been over-charging him for over 20 years. No wonder he could afford the luxury villa in the South of France!

Mr Perkins was duped into forking out for a higher price by some misguided perception of friendship, making him too afraid to question the price or ask for a discount. What was needed to get him the best deal for his grass seed was an objective view with distance from the subjective loyalty of Mr Perkins.

Think of it this way. Mr Perkins' goal was to reduce his costs, but standing in his way was his friendship with his grass seed supplier. It's like a young boy who has kicked his football over the fence into his neighbour's garden. Unfortunately, the boy is not tall enough to see over the fence. Soon enough his older brother comes out into the garden and after hearing his little brother's problem, lifts him over the fence so that he can retrieve his football.

In this analogy, the goal of retrieving his football can be likened to Mr Perkin's goal to reduce his costs. The role of Mr Perkin's friendship with his grass seed supplier is represented by the fence, which is too high for the boy to climb over. The young boy's height, or lack of it, represents Mr Perkins' subjective view. The point being that the young boy is so small that the idea of climbing over the fence doesn't even cross his mind, just as Mr Perkins' subjective view of his relationship with his 'friend' denies him the ability to consider that negotiating a discounted price with the grass seed supplier is an option.

The role of the big brother represents the outsourced company who specialises in cost reduction. Having assessed the situation the big brother decides the best option would be for him to give his younger brother a lift over the fence. It's a no-brainer! He comes to this conclusion almost immediately as his view is not restricted by a lack of height. An outsourced company is in a better position to see over the fence, as it were, and to realise the most suitable and efficient way to reduce the costs of their client.

CUTTING THROUGH THE (OFFICE) POLITICS

When an outside company is brought into an office environment they can ask all the tricky questions that were not previously being asked. This is perhaps most valuable when it comes to dealing with office politics, when the people you are potentially going to upset are the same people that you have to work with every single day.

No one wants to irritate someone they have to spend long periods of time with, especially the person who works at the opposite desk.

Everyone just wants to get along. However, difficult questions need to be asked to shake up and wake up the company from its relative state of languor. If a company is really committed to reducing its costs then this is a necessity.

"An outside company can instantly transcend the 'Oh, but I might upset him' barrier!"

These questions can be tricky because they might involve challenging the work practices of your colleagues. They might also involve adopting new unfamiliar business practices, which are a huge nuisance at first. No one is going to like someone who is making their job harder, but tough questions need to be asked.

The risk of irritating people needs to be taken and is something an outsider is better suited to do. They can afford to transcend the *'Oh, but I might upset him!'* barrier, which so often seems to hold a company's employees back.

An outside company can pose these difficult questions without it being personal, as the relationship between your company's workers and their consultants is temporary.

An outside cost reduction company offers a process of cutting through office politics, a fresh set of eyes and a fresh set of relationships.

This new approach is the key to asking all the difficult questions that simply were not being asked before.

CHALLENGING THE NORM

The CEO is an important part of this process and should be present on the board during any meetings with an outside company. Posing difficult, unsettling questions that challenge the norms of the company's business practice may annoy some of your staff.

A lot of employees will be unsettled, perhaps even angered, with the outside company's interference. Everyone likes to think they know best, especially when it comes to their company, their business practice, their job and the specific tasks they personally carry out every single day. The CEO is needed to reassure his employees that these suggestions are in the best interest of the company, as well as for each of them personally.

If the company is reducing costs, the process will increase profits leading to the expansion of the company, which will include greater perks and job security for staff. The CEO needs to reassure his staff by reminding them of what's in it for them!

By doing so he also gives the cost reduction project a much-needed authority, which will help the initiative gain momentum quickly. The CEO is also in the position to reward his employees for aiding in the cost reduction process.

Your employees might be initially sceptical about working with an outsider because they see it as an unnecessary cost. They might reason that having successfully made savings, the last thing the company needs is to fork out money by sharing savings with an outside company. They will question: *Do we really need them? Do they really need to get so much out of it?*

This scepticism is misguided and can easily be dismissed by making sure your team understands that this just isn't the case. The CEO is better placed to know the true worth of cost reduction, as he can see the overall picture. He needs to reassure his team that outside help is for the best.

Tell your staff that they need to think more carefully about what the company is actually gaining from the process, where these new savings are coming from and who has made it possible. This will show them that the company is getting great value for money.

Remember that before the outsourced company came in to help, the company wasn't making any of these savings. The equivalent amount was just being wasted.

Don't worry how much of a share the outside company will be paid because without them and their expertise there would be no share for them to take in the first place. Without them your company would still be throwing away money on needless costs.

Most companies in this field – *The Cost Reduction Company*, for instance – will work on some sort of cost-saving guaranteed basis, so you can relax. You will only be paying a fee if costs are reduced and profits are gained.

It is a win-win situation!

Your staff may think that they could have made these savings themselves, in-house, and yes the truth is that they probably could have in an ideal world. Yet, realistically, most companies simply don't allocate the time to do so.

It is important to get everyone on board and fully committed to the cost reduction strategy so that both parties can work together efficiently to get the most out of the collaboration. The CEO is responsible for making that happen!

BENCHMARKING

Benchmarking is a particularly effective way of putting your company on the right track, once again using the advantages of taking an objective view. Benchmarking is basically a means of seeing how your company runs in the light of comparison with similar companies of a similar size. Let me illustrate this with two examples.

The Cost Reduction Company was once brought in to reduce the costs of a school whose utility bills, particularly their water bill, were incredibly high. Their water bill came to a staggering £40,000 per annum. Our priority was to find out whether this cost was necessary. We do this by trying to find out what is causing the exorbitant spend and then exploring alternatives.

A simple way to evaluate a cost like this is to compare the utility bill of the school with utility bills of similar-sized schools. The comparison needs to be fair. You must make sure that the schools you are comparing are all of the same size in terms of things like number of buildings, size of buildings, number of pupils, number of staff, acres of grounds and so on.

In this particular case, it became clear that their water bill was excessive, as most schools were paying no more than £20,000 per year. We asked the school what they thought about this and they admitted they had always considered it a large cost, but were comfortable with the expenditure because they were used to paying it!

You need to avoid this kind of complacent thinking and realise the opportunity cost. The school could use this money for a whole variety of things. How about new goal posts for the football pitch or maybe some new computers for the IT department?

It was clear that something wasn't quite right. Now we needed to locate the source of the problem, which can sometimes be easier said than done. We thought it best to carry out a leak detection to see if this was the cause. This was an instant success, as we stumbled upon a leak which had been costing the school an extra £15,000 a year.

The maintenance team was actually aware of a possible leak but dismissed the noise as coming from an air conditioning unit. Now, I am not bringing this up to attribute blame but simply to highlight that this kind of error occurs in a relaxed workplace environment. Such waste will continue to happen if companies don't rigorously question their practices and seek cheaper, more efficient ways of doing things. This is why it is so important to hire an objective viewpoint.

Another example from a different school: using benchmarking, we found that the school's gas bills were almost twice as large as they should have been. So, as always, we began to investigate and noticed that out on the lawn of the school quad there was a long line of thick grass. This had annoyed the gardener for years, as every time he cut the lawn the same spot would grow back twice as fast.

We found out that a gas pipe flowed underneath and was causing this phenomenon to occur. Because the pipe was not properly lagged, it was heating the ground and causing the grass to grow at double its usual speed. Once this was sorted out, the school reduced their gas bill by a significant amount, as well as saving the gardener's time and resources.

Without using benchmarking, no one would have ever realised there was any serious wastage going on, they would have remained entirely oblivious to the situation and the gardener would have continued to quietly curse his curious lawn-mowing duties.

RELEVANT EXPERTISE

Another benefit of using an outside company who specialise in cost reduction is that they are good at it! It is their expertise. They are entirely geared toward reducing costs; it being their core business. You can be guaranteed that they know what they are doing and that they would have overcome similar obstacles to the one's facing your company before.

My company works with a lot of schools, and we are particularly efficient in this line of work. We are familiar with the ways that schools tend to waste their money, simply because we have witnessed a multitude of different schools making the same mistakes time and time again. Outside companies earn this kind of specialised knowledge through years of experience. To gain access to this kind of knowledge you need to bring in the experts. There is no other way!

Experience is everything! Just think about parenting. As a parent, you will experience a whole host of unfamiliar challenges with your first child. When the second child arrives you are better suited to deal with these problems as you can call upon the experiences of dealing with your first. Now, let's say that your eldest child does something wrong. Well, you can explain exactly what they have done wrong to the second child, as well as how to avoid making the same mistakes. You are effectively taking the experiences from one and transferring it to the other.

The same approach is taken by a company specialising in cost reduction. These experts are brought in to reduce costs at one company, find out whatever is causing them to waste money, figure out how to fix this and then know what to do if they see the same problem again. They are in a very good position, nurtured through years of experience, to assess the best ways to reduce your company's costs. And even if they find something new *to them*, they are still much better suited to identify and solve the *real* problem.

Think of it this way. You would not ask your accountant to draft your new contract. You would ask your lawyer who is an expert in this field. He has spent a lot of time doing contracts and by using his expertise you will get the best out of the service. The same goes for everything in life.

Whenever you want to get something done and need someone to do it, whether it is to draw up a contract, fly a plane, drive a bus, educate your children, play in goal for your favourite football team or perform open heart surgery, you want someone to do the job that has the relevant experience necessary to undertake the tasks involved. We would never query this division of labour in any other situation!

Cost reduction is no different!

WORKING SMART

Most businesses run on what is called a reactive basis. When confronted with the instruction: *"I need that account filed by noon!"* the average office worker will focus all their energy on getting that done as soon as is humanly possible. The immediacy of the situation launches the task up their list of priorities.

They will never think, *"How can I adhere to my strict deadline while finding extra time to find ways of reducing the cost of the procedure I am currently undertaking, whilst, all the while, reviewing other more general aspects of the company to see if costs can be made elsewhere!"* They will just get it done as quickly as possible and move onto their next task.

Reducing costs is a proactive not reactive process.

It takes a whole lot of time, and someone needs to put that time in. When an outsider comes in they will have the time that you and your employees will always struggle to find.

Thus, by hiring an outside company to reduce your costs you are effectively doing so by buying time; time that can be used to reduce your costs!

Therefore, using these outside resources allows you to **WORK SMART!** Working smart means focusing on what you are good at. It involves allocating the use of your company's precious resources to the most important priorities associated with your core business, because, at the end of the day, this is what matters. If you use your resources for some other purpose then you will end up neglecting your core business, simply because you don't have the time.

Imagine an old-fashioned shoemaker who goes into business to make shoes. To provide the best shoes on a day-to-day basis, he needs to focus all his efforts and resources into making them. He knows he can provide a better service if he could expand his business, perhaps taking on an apprentice, acquiring finer raw materials and obtaining better tools, but, to do this, he would need to find some extra money from somewhere. He realises he can do this by reducing his costs, but immediately encounters an insurmountable problem.

To reduce his costs he will need to use all the time that he usually uses to make shoes. This means that he will have to shut down the shop for a week or so and won't be able to make or sell any shoes. He won't be able to make his usual living. He may also permanently lose a large percentage of his customers as they take their business elsewhere. What he needs to do is outsource the cost reduction process.

Then, he could focus on his core business while someone else comes in to look at the state of his costs. An outside company provides him with the opportunity to work smart.

It is all about the opportunity cost of your company's time and resources. If your company is highly efficient at sales, then focus on sales. It is all about meeting the core needs of your business. You cannot fall into the trap of using up your resources on cost reduction when they could be put to better use in sales. Likewise, you know your customers so focus on satisfying them, and you know how to run your day-to-day business, so focus on that. An outside company specialises in cost reduction, so let them do that. They will do a better job than you could as they have the expertise. The idea is to save you huge costs whilst you continue to work on making profits as per usual.

CHAPTER SUMMARY

- *The two major benefits of outsourcing are an* **OBJECTIVE VIEW** *and* **TIME**

- *Outsourcing allows you to* **WORK SMART**

- *An outsider can cut through office politics*

- *Benchmarking is a great starting point*

- *A company specialised in reducing costs has the relevant specialised expertise*

- *Cost reduction is a proactive process*

Chapter Five

YOU NEED A TEAM ... AND A LEADER DRIVING THE PROCESS

Key questions:
What is the first thing to do when beginning a cost
reduction programme? What is the role of the CEO?
What are the best ways to keep employees motivated?
How do you encourage staff to get behind the cost
reduction process?

DON'T ASSUME EVERYONE LIKES ICE CREAM

Taking on a cost reduction project is a large commitment. If outsourcing doesn't appeal to you, you must be prepared to put in the effort and the hours. Unless the project is thoroughly thought through from the start and your plans are rigorously seen through to the end, the results won't be anywhere near as fruitful as anticipated. It could all end up being for nothing.

Any project of this scope is going to need a committee. Therefore, the first thing to do is elect the committee members.

Then ensure that the rest of your employees, who aren't included on the committee, understand that this doesn't mean that their input isn't just as important. Whatever the size of the organisation, everybody needs to be involved. A hardworking, well organised and, above all, motivated staff is essential.

Perhaps most importantly, you need to have the right person leading the group, overseeing the project and motivating all the personnel involved. The CEO should really take on this role. This chapter addresses the responsibilities of the CEO in encouraging and then rewarding the team in driving forward this cost reduction strategy.

Any team is made up of individuals, who all function differently and won't necessarily be motivated by the same incentives. Therefore, to be done effectively, personnel management must be regarded as a many-sided beast.

Not every child likes ice cream, but most children do. If I wanted to treat my daughter and her friends on a hot summer's day, I probably wouldn't think too hard about it and just offer them all an ice cream.

However, one of my daughter's friends doesn't like ice cream, but all the other children dive into theirs with a huge smile on their faces.

Not to worry, having appeased the majority of the group, I can now offer her something else. All I have to do is ask what she would prefer instead. Perhaps, she would like an apple. I don't know. It's just an example!

The point is that personnel management works like this. It cannot be guaranteed that any one tip or method will work for everybody. You can rest assured that it doesn't take much to motivate most, but it is highly likely that at least a few of your employees will need to be approached from a slightly different angle. Once the majority is satisfied and motivated, you can deal with the others who might not be so happy.

"A hard working, well organised and motivated staff is essential!"

THE CEO AND THE COMMITTEE

Make sure you take the time to really consider who is going to join the committee. These people will be functioning as the cornerstones of the project. Ideally, it is the department heads or specially nominated department representatives who take these positions. The most important thing is that the committee works as a means to serve the interests of the whole company.

Like everything else in business, it all comes down to communication. Excellent communication is the key to cost reduction. Everyone must know that they can and should contribute to the process. The knack here is to get the most out of what is available to you.

The department representatives must be in constant communication with everyone in their department. Aim to establish a free-flowing stream of ideas, all the way from the bottom of your company to the top. The committee is there simply to channel this proactive work ethic and creative flow of ideas into the right areas and to make sure the potential for cost reduction is actualised.

In truth, another employee could potentially take on this role – the one I am about to prescribe to the CEO – but they will never have the same authority as the CEO, and it is this authority which validates the cost reduction project and gives it impetus.

In short, the CEO has two main objectives.

Firstly, they need to ensure that costs are reduced and secondly, they need to make sure that all employees are happy. These two things overlap considerably. If the company is reducing costs it will begin to make profits and everyone will reap the rewards, creating a positive atmosphere in the office. Likewise, if your employees are happy because they see that their hard work is actually achieving substantial results – and they are personally being rewarded for these efforts – they are more likely to work even harder to reduce costs.

More specifically there are five key ways that the CEO can make sure the cost reduction project is a success.

These are:

1. Asking questions
2. Involving everybody
3. Rewarding everybody
4. Publicly displaying results
5. Finding quick wins

ASKING QUESTIONS

As the chair of the committee, the CEO has a responsibility to ask demanding questions, which are essential in launching the project and maintaining its progression. There are a number of important questions that need to be continually asked and re-asked.

Questions like:

"Do we need to do this?"
"Is this expenditure really necessary?"
"Is there a cheaper way that won't reduce quality?"
"Why are we doing it this way?"
"What are the alternatives, if any?"

It is very easy to fall back on traditions. The CEO must make sure this doesn't happen by striving to maintain a level of dynamism and innovation at all times.

This means constantly looking at ways to improve the company. If the answer to the question, *"Why are we doing it this way?"* is nothing other than *"Because we always have!"* then the next question needs to be: *"Well then, what are the possible alternatives?"* This is an easy and effective way to seek out new ways of cutting costs.

It is a natural human tendency to revert to the same old tried and tested techniques and to stand steadfast in one's traditions. For starters it is easy, as there is nothing new to learn. You may even think that it is beneficial to stick to your guns, to do the same things over and over until the end of time because *surely it costs to renovate? Surely change costs money?*

However, this kind of short-term thinking is lazy and will cost you money in the long-term. If you take the time to look, you are bound to find all sorts of cheaper alternatives to improve on your current practices. Get rid of the *'Because we always have!'* attitude and keep everyone continually questioning and improving the company's methods and business practices.

GET EVERYONE INVOLVED

Once a committee is set up it is paramount that the rest of the staff who didn't make the committee, that is, the majority of your employees, don't feel neglected. By involving as many people in the decision process as possible you are more likely to achieve camaraderie amongst your staff and the feeling that they are all part of a unit.

This will lead to a more thorough understanding of what is going on and what needs to be done, and better results will naturally follow. The responsibility once again falls on the shoulders of the CEO to get everybody involved.

First of all, it is important to dismantle the natural sense of hierarchy in the office as much as possible, so that everyone feels comfortable working together and is satisfied that their ideas will actually be listened to. Nothing will suffocate and stifle an employee's creativity as much as the feeling that their opinion is worthless. You cannot allow your employees to feel as if they are just stuck sitting at their desk, alienated from the boardroom and the decision-making process.

People often say that two heads are better than one. Well, how about a whole office full of heads. Get everyone involved!

A good idea is always a good idea regardless of who it comes from. You need to make sure that everyone knows that their ideas will be heard. Part of your role is getting the most out of your employees by creating an environment where they are happy to share their thoughts. People need to have the confidence to come forward. It is your job to empower them in this way.

Most of your savings are going to come through the middle management, which is notorious for its nervous disposition. In the current economic climate people can't help but feel under pressure, worrying that they might lose their jobs or that their colleagues are doing a better job than they are.

The idea is not to get rid of this pressure entirely, as some inter-colleague competition is a great motivational source, but to make them feel comfortable working under that pressure. Your employees need some sort of security and this can be guaranteed by making them feel like they are included and that their ideas are being heard and appreciated.

How should it be done? Well, there are many effective ways of doing this. You need to work out a way for the committee to communicate directly with the rest of the office. This is the point of electing department representatives, who are known and trusted in their particular departments, so that your employees feel comfortable coming forward to share and discuss their ideas. This way they can work on reducing costs together as a group and then propose their best ideas to the committee using the authority of their department representative.

So that people are not deterred from participating, you need to make sure that they feel they are being encouraged to get involved. To do this you must stress that by participating in the sharing of ideas your employees are aiding in the growth of the company, regardless of whether their ideas will be implemented. It is a case of no particular idea being a bad idea, that the act of not contributing will actually have more of a negative impact on the company.

SUGGESTIONS PLEASE?

There must also be some process or system, whether it is an online blog or a physical post box, which is easy to use and universally accessible to any individual who wants to suggest an idea.

In the age of high speed internet access and smart phone technology, a blog, forum or interactive social media website may be a popular, handy tool for this purpose. As it is online, people can access it whenever they want, wherever they are. Suddenly struck by a great idea on the commute to work, an employee can post it instantly before it's forgotten! All these ideas will be processed quickly by the computer and stored in one location that is easy to access.

Of course, you still need someone to monitor the website and make sure it's functioning all the time. There is nothing worse than implementing something like a blog designated for ideas and feedback and people complaining because the blog is down or hasn't been checked for a week. Your employees might worry that it is just a front, that they are still being ignored.

If time allowed, the most beneficial option would be to approach each employee on a personal basis and ask directly for ideas of how the company could reduce costs. Without the luxury of personal interviews, the suggestion box is a practical alternative.

As CEO, you will tend to spend your time looking at the big picture, and working on how to fix large-scale problems. This can leave you relatively ignorant of the everyday tasks that your employees carry out.

It is just as important to look for savings in these places.

It could be something as simple as the number of paperclips used on a particular file or filing system. An employee uses a certain number of paperclips and suggests they could get away with using less. Now you are saving money on each paper clip that you no longer need to use. This might seem like a trivial saving at first, but when you consider how many times paper-clips are used every day, every week, throughout the year, you suddenly have quite a significant saving.

WE HARNASSED THE EXCESS ENERGY OF THE YEAR 9 LADS AND CUT OUR POWER BILLS IN HALF

Little things can go a long way. Just think of Tesco's *"Every little helps."* It is a slogan that has rocketed Tesco to the front of the supermarket industry not only because it is something people can relate to but also because it is an effective philosophy – one that is the basis of cost reduction. Every small saving adds up in the end.

Each saving is as important as the next and contributes to the growth of the company.

Even though ideas proposed in this way are bound to miss the mark once in a while, make sure they are all read. It is vital that your employees know that their ideas are being considered, however insignificant some of them seem at first glance.

REWARDING EVERYBODY

Rewarding people for their contribution is the most important part of personnel management. Neglecting this can be disastrous, as your staff won't see the point of contributing if they feel their work is under-appreciated and their good ideas are being ignored. There are many ways of going about showing appreciation but, once again, communication is the key!

It is always important to get to know your staff, as much as time allows. Now by this, I don't mean getting to know every little detail about them. Don't go around imposing yourself on your staff asking them about their relationship status, whether they have kids, where they live, what car they drive and where they were born. You don't need to take each employee out to dinner or anything of the sort!

If you have a rough idea of what makes them tick and what gets them out of bed in the morning then you know how to reward them for all their hard work, and, in turn, motivate them to work even harder for you.

You just need to have a general idea of what it is that will motivate them. It is also important to note that money might not be the only form of motivation! In fact, I have found it rarely is!

Remember that no two people are the same. So make sure that everyone's desired means of being rewarded is accommodated for by giving them options. Have a system where your employees know that if they save the company expenses then they will be rewarded with either this option or that option. They have a choice.

Perhaps they want to store up their credit to earn a greater reward. So accommodate this in the system by letting them know that they have a choice to work harder on a more challenging project, for which they will be rewarded with something extra special.

"It is the CEO's authority which validates the cost reduction project and gives it impetus!"

These rewards can be anything your employees find valuable. As mentioned, it could be a holiday, a weekend away, a dinner with the CEO, a bonus, a bottle of champagne, or it could simply be recognition among their peers. Don't be scared to reward employees with pay rises and offer promotion for exceedingly good work on a consistent basis.

The *Employee of the Week* plaque has become a cliché and may not be taken seriously, yet the sentiment is still valid and effective as a motivational tool.

As long as it's done in a way that people are comfortable with, public recognition of employees' achievements will spur them on to further success and create an environment of friendly competition.

If someone has earned praise and it is publicly acknowledged, others will start to think: *"Hey, I could have done that!"* or *"I want some of that recognition. I guess I am going to have to work harder!"* As long as everyone has an equal opportunity to flourish then public recognition should work a treat.

A good way to make sure your employees know that their work is fully appreciated is some kind of written recognition. It gives the impression that you are personally grateful for their input.

Personally, I use this option all the time. I like to hand out some kind of thank you card that my employees can display at their desks. It should say something like *"Thank you for saving our company!"* or *"I have saved my company!"* It is a small token which can mean a lot, a small gesture that can go a long way. I have found that people really cherish them.

It works in the same way as a school merit system. I have found that most people enjoy this kind of challenge, seeing it as a bit of a game; however, I am aware that some people may be sceptical, claiming that they don't need childish incentives to work harder.

In the past, I have also heard people criticise these public displays of recognition by claiming they are *too American*, whatever that means.

I admit that it might not be for everyone, but I have a simple way of responding. I simply walk them around the office and show them how everybody else is collecting their cards and keeping them pinned up over their desks.

I guess it is a bit like the ice cream situation. Not everyone likes ice cream, but most people do. So don't be afraid to offer it just because a small minority might not like it. In general, people are proud to be recognised as having achieved. As CEO, use this to your advantage to keep up morale and provide that extra motivation!

RECORD SAVINGS AND PUBLICLY DISPLAY THEM

In a similar vein, your employees will be more motivated if they know that their efforts are achieving results. So make them public! Put up a record of your results in the office for everyone to see. Update it as soon as goals are reached and savings are made.

There are many computer programs that will do this for you, but a cheap way of doing it is to use a drawing of a thermometer, for example. Any progress can be shaded in with no effort at all.

First, you need to make sure that your employees' goals are clearly defined.

Let us use an example of a company that provides cricket tours. In the next six months the business wants to make £75,000 worth of savings. Acknowledge that so far the company has made savings of £10,000.

On the thermometer, put £75,000 at the top and place a mark for every £5,000 leading up to it. Straight away you can colour in up to £10,000 so everyone can see that you are already on the way to succeeding in this goal.

You might prefer to quantify the thermometer in a way that your employees are more likely to relate to. A good thing to do is to define the goal in terms of what is most important for the company. So in this case, we are defining the savings in terms of tours saved as this is what is important to the company. This way your staff knows exactly what they are working for. Each tour costs £25,000.

So let's redefine it by saying for the next six months we want to save three tours, as this is the equivalent of £75,000. Now when a saving is made, the amount saved – let's say £12,000 – is added to the running total – now at £22,000 – and you can colour in the thermometer up to that amount so your staff can quickly see the result of their hard work.

They will also be motivated by the fact that they now only have to save £3,000 to save one tour, which doesn't seem so intimidating. This use of public measurement will get people working together toward their combined goal.

Feedback needs to be given to employees on a weekly or monthly basis so that everyone has this information and can get on top of their goals. These kinds of things are used in sales all the time when people have weekly or daily goals to meet.

When it is visualised as clear as this, no one can have any excuses if they under perform. They know what the consequences are if they don't sell enough.

For some reason you rarely see this approach used in cost reduction. There is no reason why this model shouldn't be used in this way. It works all the same.

Of course, the cricket tours company was just used as an example and the thermometer diagram can be applied to anything. Just remember that you need to think about what is of most importance and define your savings in terms of these goals.

With a school, for instance, you could quantify the thermometer in terms of hardship bursaries. Many schools want to offer these scholarships but can't afford to as much as they would like. By knowing that saving £x will provide five students with bursaries is more likely to motivate them to find new ways of reducing costs and making savings.

FINDING QUICK WINS

Not everybody will be keen on the initiative at the outset. Without the full cooperation of the whole body of staff you will miss out on savings. One handy way to gain momentum is to find and identify **QUICK WINS** to prove the worth of the concept.

Your employees may be sceptical. They might think nothing is wrong with how things are already done: *"Just let me get on with my job!"* Remember, we need to get rid of the *'Because we have always!'* attitude. Instantly prove the worth of the initiative by picking something easy to begin with.

It could be something that you have been meaning to do for a long time, but haven't found the time to get around to. Maybe you have known for a while that you could make a quick saving by switching internet provider, but never felt the sufficient motivation to make the change. It hasn't been a priority.

Now is the perfect time to get around to it. If it's an easy way to get a quick win in the bag, do it. This way the cost reduction strategy will get instant backing from the staff and quickly gain forward momentum.

People will also be more forthcoming with their ideas if they see that costs can be reduced with such ease. You want to encourage an environment where people are thinking: "I could have thought of that, how about this idea!"

CHAPTER SUMMARY

- *The CEO will add authority to the project*

- *The CEO must ask difficult questions*

- *Create a committee by selecting department representatives*

- *All staff need to be involved*

- *Publicly display results*

- *Quantify and display results in terms of what is most important to your company or staff*

- *Find quick wins to gain momentum*

Chapter Six

THE IMPORTANCE OF SPECIFICATION

Key questions:
What is the specification? What is the importance of the specification? What can you do to ensure the quality of your specification? What can go wrong and how can this be avoided?

THE SPECIFICATION

The **SPECIFICATION** is what is expected when providing a product or service to a customer.

An important way of reducing costs is taking the time to ensure that all parties involved are absolutely clear about what is going on and what is expected from them. This is all down to communication. Something as simple as neglecting to ask a particular question can cause your company unnecessary costs. So it is absolutely vital that you are thorough in defining exactly what you desire from the product or service.

It is just a process of defining what is really happening and asking all the right questions. If you outline a high quality specification you are in control.

There will be no unexpected turn of events that will affect your pricing. In this chapter I shall cover:

1. Defining the product
2. Defining the service
3. Involving all parties in the design of the specification
4. How and when it can go wrong

The real incentive for taking time to ensure you have a quality specification is ensuring a level of **CONTROL** over your business. It is important that you are fully aware of what is going on at all times. Every time you enter any kind of business transaction you must feel, first of all, that you are getting what you want and need and, second of all, you are doing so in a way that is going to benefit your company, that is, getting the best deal or price available. The best way to do this is to make sure your supplier knows exactly what you want.

It becomes an issue of control: control over what you are getting, physically, and control over how much you are willing to pay. If you fail to do this then you will become reliant on your supplier and will lose control of your pricing.

"Reducing costs really can be as simple as asking a question which had not previously been asked!"

A good supplier should automatically help in these situations. It's to their advantage that costs are kept to a minimum and that a strong business relationship is maintained by all parties. However, it is very dangerous if you do become overly reliant on your supplier. Remember that they have a business to run just as much as you do, and will be trying to get the most out of the deal as well.

Let's think about specification in terms of buying a laptop and imagine you are so busy with work that you have asked me to buy one for you. A laptop can come in all different shapes and sizes, brands and types. Also there is a whole load of variables that determine its performance, and the price of the laptop is effectively determined by performance – of course, branding plays a part too.

The performance of a laptop is determined by a range of components such as the processor, the memory, the drive, the graphics cards, the screen resolution etc. I also need to know what will be your primary use for your laptop. Is it for work, for watching DVDs, for streaming online videos, for gaming, for family use?

Again there are other things to consider like any software that might be included, the length and extent of warranty, as well as all those extra bits and bobs that the salesman always tries to dump on you at the last minute. These are all factors that need to be considered when defining the specification.

The goal is to make sure that we are both agreed on what it is you want. If we don't undertake this with a great deal of precision, I am likely to disappoint you.

I could rush out and buy a brand new high performance *Macbook Pro*, splashing out a cool £1,000, when you wanted nothing of the sort and were ideally just after *any-old-thing* that could browse the internet and play Solitaire without stalling every 20 seconds.

Likewise, I might present you with a laptop that doesn't include software you would have liked, like *Microsoft Word* for instance. If this is the case, I will have to return to the shop or, worse still, you might have to go yourself. Now this will, in all likelihood, be a massive inconvenience to you, considering that it was because you were so busy that you had asked me to buy the laptop for you in the first place. You will also have to incur an additional cost as you have to buy *Microsoft Word* separately, a cost you had expected to be included in the package. So there are a lot of things that can quickly go wrong if the specification is not thoroughly defined.

Now it seems more than likely that, in such a scenario, you would automatically make sure that I knew what kind of laptop you wanted. However, it is easy to imagine where taking such a precaution might slip the mind.

A busy organisation like a school will be focused primarily on its core business – providing its pupils with the highest standard of education possible. A task like buying stationery will be overshadowed by greater priorities and may fade into insignificance. A school will be more anxious about ensuring that it has the best teachers, classrooms and other facilities.

Staff will also be preoccupied with the day-to-day running of the school, making sure that utility bills and wages are paid on time. A school in the 21st century is pretty useless without electricity! Something like buying geometry sets will find itself a lot further down the list of priorities.

However, it can be a huge error to take less care defining the specification for something just because it's thought of as a low priority. When anything is bought in bulk, not taking care to have a quality specification can lead to large costs that are completely unnecessary.

What is true of a product is also true of a service. You must make sure that the service being provided is thoroughly defined and understood by all parties involved. An example I often refer to when discussing this involves a friend of mine, who runs a hotel. He appealed to a company who claimed that they could reduce his running costs by 15%, which equated to something like £45,000-£50,000, a very significant sum.

The company sent someone over to his hotel to assess his situation and spent a few weeks providing the necessary work that was the initial part of the service. They focused on the volume of alcohol that the hotel went through and the specific wines, beers and spirits that the hotel bar offered, including the prices as well as the popularity of each beverage as indicated by the amount consumed by the clientele. This process lasted for three weeks as they collected all the information they needed.

Finally, the day arrived when the outside company was to present their findings and the means by which they would reduce the running costs of the hotel. They suggested a cost reducing strategy that involved delivering the hotel's supply of alcohol on a fortnightly basis, pointing out that the hotel would receive a large discount by changing the delivery schedule.

My hotelier friend automatically had to reject this recommendation, as his cellar wasn't big enough to carry the sheer amount of stock that would amass with a fortnightly delivery. He needed stock to be delivered daily. He had no intention of enlarging his cellar as he simply couldn't afford to renovate. When this was finally established, it turned out the 15% savings originally quoted would have to be dramatically reduced as daily delivery did not qualify for any discount.

All in all, bringing in the outside company cost my hotelier friend three weeks of work for absolutely no return and could have been avoided if he had taken the precaution of making more of an effort to define the service that was being provided at the outset.

The whole problem was born from a lack of communication between the two parties. Now, a story like this clearly emphasises how important it is to arrive at a quality specification; the key to which is excellent communication. It is imperative to ask the questions that would clear up a misunderstanding like this. It will save you money.

NO NEED TO DO EVERYTHING ON YOUR OWN!

You always need to be thinking in terms of what else you can do to ensure you have a quality specification. A great way to do this is to look at bringing all parts of the **SUPPLY CHAIN** into the initial design of the specification. You never know what advantages you may gain from including the supplier, the manufacturer or the end user in this process.

There are two benefits of doing this.

First, by bringing them in at this initial stage, you can make sure you have asked all the right questions from the get-go and that everyone is absolutely clear on the product or service being provided. It will ensure the quality of the specification and avoid any troubles that might spring directly from miscommunication.

Second, it allows room for suggestions, improvements and different points of view that you may not have considered yourself. The guy who is in charge and oversees the manufacturing of a product is going to know more about the intricate details and various processes that go into the manufacturing than anyone else. He will be better positioned to know if there are cheaper alternatives he can offer you at that stage of the process.

Essentially, it is a way of tapping into this expertise. You are gaining the insight of an expert. It also ensures that you have all the bases covered, which is arguably never a bad thing.

ASK THE EXPERTS:
THE SUPPLIER

Why not involve the supplier? Ask your supplier: *"How can you do this cheaper? What other options are available?"*

WHAT A STARTING POINT! If you go to the supplier and say, *"How can I reduce my price with your service?"* you are immediately creating the opportunity for him to offer a better deal. He might say that there is no room for a reduction in price. At least you have tried! Now you have the option to go ahead with the price as it is or you can go away and investigate other suppliers to discover if there are any cheaper prices out there.

However, your supplier might have something constructive to suggest. He might say, *"Well, at the moment you receive deliveries seven days a week. If you choose not to have a delivery on the weekend it will be much cheaper."* Now all you have to do is accommodate a slight increase in stock and your costs have already been reduced.

Say you are refurbishing a restaurant and planning to install a new floor. You have come up with a design that includes replacing the current vinyl flooring with wooden floor planks that are 18 inches wide. When you visit the supplier, you take the time to show him the design and ask if there is any way this job could be done cheaper. He says you can reduce the price by almost 25% by using 16 inch wide planks, because these narrower planks are straight off the shelf.

If you don't ask, you won't benefit from this inside information. Communicating your needs is about giving your supplier the opportunity to help you out.

Now, you can't just expect your supplier to jump at the chance to offer you cheap prices for nothing in return. You cannot expect this kind of altruistic behaviour. Remember that they are running a business too. Don't approach them with demands. It is more a question of enquiring, negotiating and asking for advice, *"How would you supply it cheaper?"*

There is an important difference.

The point of involving your supplier in the design of the specification is to improve the relationship between the two of you by working together to find a way that you can both benefit from this partnership now and in the future.

The more effort you make to communicate with your supplier the greater the chance they will help you reduce your costs. A great way of doing this is organising a supplier day, a day where you bring potential suppliers together to discuss possibilities for cost reduction.

Choose a decent hotel, put on a lunch and make sure everyone feels welcome. The idea is that by sitting down in a more relaxed setting, away from the workplace, you can all work together to help each other out. You start by breaking everyone up into smaller groups and sitting them around a table and asking them how they might be able to reduce the cost of their product or service.

You can use the social day to assess which suppliers you would most prefer to work with. You can also use the time to work one-to-one with your guests to discuss how you can help each other out.

But remember, it is not just for your benefit. You are giving your suppliers something back, not just a free lunch, but the chance to voice their ideas, receive feedback and, ultimately, to use what they learn to reduce their running costs.

"It is about giving your supplier the opportunity to help you out!"

There are more ideas on organising a successful supplier day in chapter nine: *Working with your supplier.*

ASK THE EXPERTS: THE MANUFACTURER

Say, for instance, that your company sells toys that consist of parts including a nut and bolt. Because of this, the cost of manufacturing will be determined by the degree of tolerance, which is the physical size of the space between the nut and the bolt.

At the moment, each individual toy costs £4.50 to manufacture because it's being produced with a tolerance of a particular degree. After asking your manufacturer about reducing the cost, you find that the toy could be produced with a degree of tolerance that is significantly cheaper.

Reducing costs really can be as simple as asking a question that had not previously been asked.

I was working recently with a company that sold aluminium wheels. The manufacturing of these wheels involved two phases. The first phase was undertaken by one company at their factory at one location where the aluminium part of the wheel was forged together. The second part was the addition of a nylon covering on both sides of the wheel, which was undertaken by a different company at a different location.

So the aluminium wheels had to be transported from the factory where they were originally manufactured to the factory where the nylon covering was secured and then all the way back to the first factory, a process that incurred a substantial cost in transport and logistics.

When I was walking around the factory floor of the first company – where my client was supplied with the aluminium wheels – I found that they also had the facilities to produce the nylon covering at the same site. In fact, they provided this service to the majority of their clients. I asked if they could do it for my client and they said, *"Of course!"* When I asked why they weren't doing it already, they said that it wasn't included in the original order.

My client was able to cancel the contract with the second company and consolidate the two phases of the process. Now, because they weren't transporting these aluminium wheels from factory to factory, they could enjoy a significant cost reduction.

A simple miscommunication like this at the outset of the contract can cost your company a lot of money.

INVOLVE THE END USER

The end user is rarely included in the design of the specification, which seems strange considering that it's the end user who will be enjoying the product your company provides. They are the consumers who will be satisfied or dissatisfied with what you are offering. By asking their opinion of your product, you are once again ensuring the quality of the specification.

If you take your product to potential customers and allow them to test your product, you can ask them if it suits their needs, if they would expect more or less from a product such as this, and if and how they would change it if they could. If your company is producing a product that has a 'high spec', you may find that you can reduce your costs because the end user would be satisfied with a product that has a 'lower spec'.

You can use customer feedback to modify products, assess the success or failure of products and to guide future thinking and design.

DON'T BE CAUGHT OUT BY THE SMALL PRINT!

The procedure of defining the specification includes knowing exactly what is written in the contract. The contract should be seen as the guarantee of the specification agreed upon.

If there is anything in there that is unclear, has been missed out or that you have failed to notice then you are taking unnecessary risks that could result in unnecessary costs.

There's a whole host of things to be concerned about here – some companies will try and get away with anything! But the key point is the need to be thorough. You need to check and then double check the content of your contract, as many companies will use the contract to try to catch you out.

"A lot of companies will include various tricks in the contract to try to catch you out!"

There are businesses that will draw up the contract with the intention of gaining an advantage over you. This quite often takes the form of a deliberate inclusion of an ambiguous phrase or word, or the slipping in of deceptive or misleading paragraphs. Looking out for this should be seen as a principal part of defining the specification.

The effect that a contract has further down the line is just as important as its immediate implications. You can reduce your costs simply by making sure you know what you are getting your company into, both in the short run and long run.

Photocopying companies are notorious for pulling this kind of scam. They will often disguise the long-term consequences of their contracts.

The last thing you want is for your company to be hit by a sudden increase in photocopying costs because you failed to notice the inclusion of small print stating that the price rises significantly at the end of each year. Overnight your photocopying cost could double.

Look out for vague definitions of what you are paying for. For instance, when a photocopier produces a copy it flashes a green light called a *'pass'.* A photocopying company may base their price upon the number of passes rather than on how many copies it produces.

So a pass may cost 5p. And 5p per copy is a price you are happy to pay. However, photocopying machines all function differently. The one you have bought may take a number of passes to make a single copy. The contract may be written to disguise this fact and, if you are not careful, you may be held to a price that costs you three times more than the amount you thought you had initially signed on for.

Taking the precaution of checking for these tricks is an effective way of reducing your costs. You must make sure that the specification is defined in terms that you understand and are comfortable with, and then you can feel reassured that the contract legally protects your interests.

THINKING ABOUT BILLING

An easy way to reduce your costs is to make sure you know what billing options are available and really take the time and effort to investigate which option will be more practical and beneficial for your company. This should be seen as part of the specification.

Invoices can add up to a significant sum and may be unnecessary. There are other options. Of course, invoices will take much longer to process if not done electronically. You need to weigh up the pros and cons. It is important to know how, when, and what you are going to be charged. By keeping on top of this information you are once again ensuring you stay in control and avoid unnecessary costs.

THINKING ABOUT DELIVERY OPTIONS

Taking the time to seek a delivery option that suits your business operations can save costs. I often see schools overlooking the importance of this. Much like any other business, a school consists of different departments. However, depending on the size of the school grounds, these departments can be located quite far apart from each other, unlike in an office, where two departments might be close by.

Imagine that a school orders all its stationery from one particular supplier. Once delivered, this stationery needs to find its way to the English Department, the Maths Department, the Bursar's Office and the Sports Centre. The deliveryman might just drop the whole order at the front desk, leaving the school with the job of distributing supplies to the different departments.

This is going to cost money. This job might be allocated to the secretary or a teaching assistant. If the school chooses this option, it will lose the time this employee could have utilised doing their usual job.

A better option could be to introduce a new 'Head of Stationery' position to distribute the supplies around the school. Either way, it is going to cost the school to distribute the stationery.

The deliveryman might offer a service to deliver to more than one location, something that wouldn't be difficult and would save the school the needless cost of employing someone for the task.

If it's outlined in the specification that the delivery will be split so that a bundle of stock is delivered to the Sports Centre, another bundle to the Bursar's Office, another to the Maths Department and so on, then the school is effectively saving the equivalent cost of a whole person. The staff member can be employed elsewhere to do a more useful job.

It is often the case that a delivery on a Saturday or Sunday will be more expensive than a delivery in the working week. If you are receiving a one-off delivery or need a long-running repeat order delivered once a week, you need to ensure you are not setting up weekend deliveries.

If you need to have something delivered on a Sunday then it is worth asking your supplier if there is any way you can reduce the cost. If your delivery is five days a week then ensure that you receive it from Monday to Friday. Or if you have to have new stock delivered seven days a week, ask your supplier if there are cheaper options, perhaps they could deliver the whole amount for the weekend on a Friday. Make sure these cost-saving concerns are addressed in the specification.

CHEAP VERSUS VALUE

If something sounds too good to be true, it's because it often is. For instance, a company approaches you with an offer of saving 20% on the cost of a certain product by finding you a different supplier.

Without any further investigation, without properly discussing what you need, you give the go ahead, as you are temporarily seduced by the lure of the 20% savings. If you had taken the time to ask them a question or two about the product, you would have found out that the new supplier was offering you a cheaper price because they were providing you with cheaper goods.

If an item is bought cheap, it means that it has been manufactured cheaply and is, therefore, more liable to break. A broken piece of kit needs to be fixed or replaced, and this is going to cost money and time as you will have to deal with the returning customer and their complaint and then undertake action to fix the problem.

A situation like this can be avoided by taking the time to attain a quality specification.

CHAPTER SUMMARY

- *The specification is what is expected when providing a product or service to a customer*

- *A quality specification will guarantee control over your business*

- *Bring in the whole supply chain*

- *Allow your supplier to help reduce your price*

- *Include the manufacturer and the end user*

- *The contract is the guarantee of the specification*

- *Work out delivery options that suits the way your business operates*

Chapter Seven

VALUE IS MORE THAN JUST 'CHEAP'

Key questions:
What is value? What is the difference between value and cheap? What does it mean to start thinking in terms of what is valuable to your company?

WHAT IS VALUABLE TO US?

There is a whole lot more to reducing costs than seeking out cheaper alternatives to your current pricing. This is because cheap is usually cheap for a reason. What you need is **VALUE.**

Now the term 'value' is variable, so what do we mean by this word? First of all, what's most important is starting to think in terms of what is valuable to you, that is, ask the questions: *"What are we looking for? What will benefit us the most?"* Value is subjective to your company and to your goal of providing a satisfactory product or service to your customers.

You want to do it right, not cheap. Yes, you want to reduce prices, but remember the end goal is to increase profits. A large part of making sales and profits is due to repeat business and the overall image of the company. This comes down to customer satisfaction, which is dependent upon the quality of the product.

You don't just want to get things done as cheaply as possible; you want to do it the right way. This way you know your product or service will fulfil the needs and expectations of the customer, and they will use your company again the next time they need what your company provides.

Of course, this really depends on your product and the demographic your product is aimed at. In most cases people prefer greater quality as long as the price is not exorbitant. However, this probably cannot be said for students, who spend their afternoons scrutinising the offerings in discount aisles. For consumers on a low income, what qualifies as the 'best value' is often the absolute cheapest, regardless of quality.

You need to know all about your product, know all about your customer base and then, with the help of rigorous and thorough market research, you will be able to figure out what 'value' means to you and your customers.

"There is a whole lot more to reducing costs than seeking out cheaper alternatives to your current pricing!"

THE POUND SHOP

If you do decide to buy cheap you must assume that your product will be lacking in quality.

Just think of the *Pound Shop*, which sells goods at unbeatably cheap prices but does so by providing goods that are usually lacking in quality. If you purchase something at a cheaper price it usually means it was manufactured for cheaper, perhaps by using cheap parts, inexperienced workers or taking short cuts in production. The chances are that the product won't be very good.

It will cost you more in the long-term if your products are liable to break. You will be forced to deal with returning customers and complaints and miss out on repeat business. You are also likely to generate a bad name for your company, gaining a reputation for poor quality.

Part of the issue about value is **PERCEPTION**. You need to think about what the quality of your product is saying about you. It can be worthwhile spending that little bit more to obtain quality that will save you money in the long-term. Choosing quality will also give your company a more credible name. There is nothing more damaging than having a reputation for a poor product. Cheap may save you money in the short-term, but having a reputation for being cheap will cost you in the long-run.

Let's look at an example. Your marketing department is looking at producing some new company umbrellas.

You decide to go for a model of umbrella that costs £5 more than the standard. For the next year all your clients will be using your umbrella rather than the cheap ones they received from your competitors.

This is good for you in two ways. First, your company's name is visible every time they open their umbrella and walk around town, which, due to the high performance of your umbrella, will be for the whole year and not just for the first few rainy days of September. This will work as advertising to attract new clients and get your company's name out on the street.

Second, it will forge a better impression of your company. Clients will appreciate that you have made an extra effort to provide a sturdy umbrella that actually works and will assume that this ethos of 'going the extra mile' abounds throughout your company. Also, every time it rains, which is a lot in this country, your client will think positively about your company.

So consider what you want from your product. In this case, what was needed was longevity, not cheap as chips. So forking out for a better model is excellent value because you are essentially buying yourself a greater chance of repeat business.

However, there is an exception to the *"Pound Store equals cheap for a reason"* argument. If what you are buying is a branded good then you are guaranteed quality. If I am buying a Mars bar, I know that I am getting a Mars bar. You are guaranteed quality and therefore know that by buying it for a cheaper price at the *Pound Shop* you are getting good value.

It becomes a viable purchase. This exception to the rule is something to think about when looking at buying cheap goods.

THE REAL VALUE

So, in a general sense, the **REAL VALUE** of something is the value as seen in terms of its relative worth to you. Value can also be defined as *"The worth of something relative to the price paid."*

If you are dining out and the main meal costs £14.95 you may believe this price is expensive in *The Unicorn*, a cheap and cheerful pub, but not expensive in *The Crooked Billet*, a posh gastro pub.

In the gastro pub you are happy to spend £14.95 and see it as value for money. Again, this is to do with guaranteed quality, like with the branded product in the *Pound Shop,* but also down to perception and taste. There are certain things, like the quality of ingredients, service from the staff, stylish atmosphere and general ambience, lighting, mood, and background music, which are to your liking.

But the guarantee comes from the fact that it is generally perceived as being a critically acclaimed restaurant, having received excellent reviews in the local paper or perhaps you know that it is hard to get a table in there on a Friday or Saturday night. So the important thing is to think in terms of value, rather than cheap.

"Value is the worth of something relative to the price paid". So, somewhere in the balancing act of **COST** and **QUALITY** lies **VALUE.**

One final note: If all goes well and you have written your specification to ensure the product or service is what you require, then the price you get becomes value to you!

CHAPTER SUMMARY

- *There is more to reducing costs than seeking out cheaper alternatives to your current pricing.*

- *What you need is value.*

- *Cheap is usually cheap for a reason.*

- *What is the quality of your product saying about your company?*

- *Poor quality risks upsetting customer satisfaction and losing repeat business.*

Chapter Eight

USING MEASUREMENT TO DELIVER YOUR 'GOAL'

Key questions:
How will measurement help your company reduce its costs? How can you use measurement to improve the performance of employees?

CLARIFICATION THROUGH COMMUNICATION

At the beginning of any company initiative, whether it is a cost reduction programme or anything else, you need to make sure your staff is 100% clear on three things:

1. The goals of the company
2. How these goals are going to be achieved
3. What role they have to play in this

"Everybody needs to be on board and know exactly what is going on!"

Issuing explicitly defined **TARGETS** and **GOALS** is the best way to establish clarity amongst workers. At the outset, the cost reduction process can seem like a daunting task. It might also appear abstract to your employees unless they are set realistic targets and given a plan on how to reach these targets.

MEASUREMENT becomes a large part of this. Let your employees know that, as of today, we have saved £x, but, by the end of the month, we must meet our target of £y. I have mentioned in previous chapters the thermometer method of recording savings,  but this could also be done using live screens. Using something like this sets your staff with a target that is visually represented and, therefore, spelt out in the simplest of terms.

IMPROVING PERFORMANCE WITH MEASUREMENT

This kind of thing is used a lot in sales, primarily, to measure employee performance, but also because it's easier for your staff to motivate themselves when they are aware – being constantly reminded – of their personal targets and how close they are to reaching them. *"I still have 20 units to sell this week or the boss is going to be angry!"*

By using measurement like this, you instantly know how well your staff members are doing, or how badly. What is so efficient about this method is the fact information is constantly relayed back to workers. Measurement has the same effect when used in relation to cost reduction. It is a great motivator and will spur on your employees.

Measurement is also a way of saying: *"This is the focus! This is what is really important! This is what we are trying to do! So, think hard about what you can do to help!"* It is important to keep it up. You have to be constantly letting staff know what you expect from them, measuring them, feeding back how they are doing and measuring them again. This will result in dramatic improvements.

The starting point of any cost reduction programme is to analyse and present employees with the current financial state and shape of the company. You need to articulate: *"This is what we are currently spending!"* and then draw a line there. This line is the starting point; the beginning of a new frontier.

The next step is to define the goal you want to achieve. This needs to be a financial figure, as well as include what you are going to spend the saving on. Something like: *"We need to save £150,000 and we will redirect the money into the new machinery we have been looking to buy for the last three years. This machinery will improve our productivity by 20% and, therefore, will also increase our company bonuses."*

This statement should be emailed to everybody. It could even be printed out and blown up as a big poster and placed in the office for everyone to see.

Place the poster by the entrance so that every time your employees arrive at work they can see their goals as a written manifesto.

Such a manifesto also gives your staff an **INCENTIVE.** The bold statement spells out the long-term benefits of reaching your shared target, not just for the benefit of the company but for your employees too. Define goals in terms of personal benefit. So, you must let them know that the company's aim is to save £150,000 and explain what this will mean for them in tangible terms, such as:

> If the company is making more money you can expect an improvement to the workplace and working conditions!

> You can expect better bonuses and salaries!

> You can expect better gifts and rewards as recognition for hard work!

Essentially you are saying to your staff: "First, we all need to work hard for the sake of the company, but then, it is all employees who will reap the rewards!" You need to give your staff an incentive to burst out of the blocks!

"It needs to be clear that this is where we are, this is where we want to be and this is how we will get there!"

USE A SPREADSHEET

A great way of representing this data is to use a spreadsheet. You need to draw up a spreadsheet with the current expenditure in the areas you want to reduce costs in. This document will provide easy access to all the relevant and important information.

It is imperative you don't leave out anything. You need to make sure you have a list of expenditures from all areas of the business. You may have stationery costs in several different departments, where some departments are buying from different suppliers. So ensure that you have covered all areas and put all the relevant costs and volumes onto your spreadsheet.

One column should show how much you are spending, and another how much you are using. Again this is just another way of making it easy for everyone to understand the situation. It is clarification through open and transparent communication. The information is there for everybody to see. What is needed next is the analysis.

WHO IS USING WHAT AND WHY?

Now that you have a spreadsheet giving you a breakdown of your volumes, you can use this to identify which departments are using more resources than others. It allows you to assess if any particular usage is warranted or just being wasted. It is essential that you make a **FAIR** judgment. If you are measuring the electricity usage of different departments, there are a number of things to consider.

Most pertinently, you have to ensure you are comparing **LIKE FOR LIKE.**

Say, for instance, that each department has its own building, you need to take into account the number of people who work in each building, the ages of building, the energy efficiency of each building relative to each other etc. If you make allowances fairly, everyone can feel as if they are competing on a level playing field.

This gives you the opportunity to assess the consumption between different departments. You may find that the electronics department is using 50% of your total consumption, whereas another department might only be using 20%. There may be a good reason for this – they may be working much harder! It could, however, be superfluous and down to bad practice.

By looking at the figures, you can find out what is really going on, and deal with it. I have seen this situation with school housemasters. One housemaster finds he has a significantly higher utility bill and blames his older building. Investigate this claim and test whether the age of the building is having a substantial effect on consumption. If this is the case, then the school needs to show more clemency with this building's consumption and allocate a larger budget for him than the budgets specified for his colleagues who have more energy efficient buildings. It's only fair!

Taking the time and effort to measure and analyse your company's current consumption gives you the opportunity to ask these questions and find out what's really going on. With a true indication of consumption, you can make the right decisions to reduce your costs and move the company onwards and upwards.

BURSTING OUT OF THE BLOCKS!

It needs to be clear to your employees that this is where we are, this is where we want to be and this is how we will get there!

You need to give your staff the necessary tools to help them reduce costs. This can be anything, as long as it gets the job done. It might just be the permission to talk openly and directly about how to save money. It might be setting aside an hour of office time for discussion. It might be allocating an hour of your own time to listen to their ideas and making sure their ideas are delivered back.

It is very important at this stage to pick the **QUICK WIN,** so you can show success to your staff and get some momentum going.

For instance, you already know you are overpaying for catering. Pick that issue first because you know it's an easy win and cutbacks won't affect the staff too much.

Once you know how much you are spending and the volume of goods you are using, you can draw up a quality specification.

CHAPTER SUMMARY

• *Measurement allows you to ask the right questions*

• *Outline the current financial state of the company*

• *Use spreadsheets*

• *Clearly define your goal and targets*

• *Redefine these in terms that will be understood*

• *Be fair: measure like for like*

Chapter Nine

WORKING WITH YOUR SUPPLIERS

Key questions:
How can you improve your relationship with suppliers?
What effect will this have on costs? What is a 'Supplier
Day'? What are the benefits of organising a Supplier
Day? What kind of things need to be considered when
organising a Supplier Day?

GIVE AND TAKE

In Chapter Four on Outsourcing, I briefly addressed one way that a poor relationship with your supplier can damage your business. To recap, in the example of Mr Perkins and his grass seed supplier, Mr Perkins was afraid to risk shaking up the friendship and so continued to pay a price for his grass seed that was unnecessarily excessive. An outside company can automatically sort out such impasses.

However, there is absolutely no reason why you shouldn't feel comfortable to renegotiate with suppliers yourself. I will demonstrate the importance of acknowledging that a healthy relationship between you and your supplier, that is, one that is best for your business, should be seen as **GIVE AND TAKE.**

When the relationship between you and your supplier is poor, mountains will be made out of molehills. Problems will arise that could and should have been dealt with easily. Direct communication is the key.

I often find that my clients are losing out in this way. I remember one client who was eager to tell us how happy they were with their existing supplier and the price and quality provided. Generally, they thought the service was excellent. When we asked the supplier if there was anything he could do to reduce the price, he immediately responded that if he was given a long-term contract he could reduce the price. I asked why he didn't have one already and he responded that my client was not willing to issue him one.

When we brought this up with the client, they claimed the complete opposite. They said that they would love to give him a contract, but they didn't think that he wanted one. As soon as the contract was sorted out the supplier reduced his price by 17.5% and the company could enjoy a reduction in their annual bill of £40,000 for the duration of the three-year contract.

Your supplier needs you just as much as you need him! If the relationship between you and your supplier is good it can be advantageous to both of you. By working closely together you can find the **RIGHT PROFIT.**

"The aim is to work closely with your supplier to find the right profit!"

What do I mean by this? Well, there is nothing to be gained in the long-term by trying to screw over your suppliers. You need to make sure they are happy with the profit you are making from utilising their services and likewise you need to be happy with the profit they are making.

It is a two-way relationship, where both parties are looking to gain an advantage over their competitors and to make as much profit as possible. By working together to achieve the right profit you are more likely to achieve this.

WORK AT THE RELATIONSHIP

There are many ways to forge a great relationship with your supplier. An easy way to do this is to include them in office parties. An invitation to your Christmas party can go a long way. If you feel they would appreciate being taken out to dinner then don't be afraid to extend the invitation. On these occasions, as well as entertaining them, you have a great opportunity to discuss how you can both get the most out of your collaboration. You can use these opportunities to work at improving how things are done at both of your companies.

The idea is to develop the kind of relationship where you know that you can count on them.

It helps if you know that your supplier will give you a piggyback if you ever need help!

It is also important to make sure they are not using you and taking your generosity and goodwill for granted. Encourage them to let you in on whatever inside information or industry tips they might have. They could fix you up with valuable contacts. All these things will help to bring in the best products available.

Whenever the situation allows, encourage them to buy from you. It doesn't have to be the case that it's only you buying from them. I am sure there is something that your company offers that they could use. Get them spending money with your company. Get them to help you out.

THE SUPPLIER DAY

I have previously mentioned the benefit of organising a *Supplier Day*. Let me reiterate this point in greater detail on how this actually works, the specific ways it can benefit your company and what putting on a *Supplier Day* demands of you.

You can set up the *Supplier Day* with two focuses in mind. You can use it to bring various suppliers of the same product together in one place to discuss how that particular product can be made to best suit your needs. This can point you in the right direction in terms of who you would or wouldn't like to work with in the future as you will be hearing who has the best ideas, first hand, allowing you to judge who seems most committed to the idea of cost reduction.

You can also use it to bring together suppliers of different commodities to discuss more general topics that will lead to a greater understanding of how the relationship between you and your supplier can affect your company's profits and efficiencies. Both of these can be incredibly effective if organised and carried out with a great degree of care and effort.

In terms of formalities, you need to make sure that your invitation includes an agenda and timeframe so that your suppliers know what to expect and how long the event will run. They are more likely to turn up if they know what is in store for them. The process can be improved dramatically by sending a questionnaire to your suppliers with the invitation so that you have a rough idea of what your guests think about certain issues. You can use their answers to plan the agenda and direct the discussion.

Choose a decent hotel, put on a lunch and make sure everyone feels welcome. The idea is that by sitting down in a more relaxed setting, away from the workplace, you can all work together to help each other out. It is all about learning through sharing ideas, and giving and receiving feedback. The day should consist of larger group discussions, as well as one-to-one sessions where you can probe further into the more interesting ideas that have surfaced through the group discussions.

Effectively, you are gaining vital knowledge to help you decide which suppliers are more likely to support you in your pursuit of cost reduction. But it is not a one-way deal, as you are giving your suppliers something back. By this I don't just mean the free lunch!

You are giving them the chance to voice their ideas, receive feedback, to feel a part of something and to reduce their running costs. You are giving them the chance to hear how other companies run. If they hear just one or two tips on how to reduce their costs from someone at the *Supplier Day* and choose to implement this, you may find this win is reflected in the future prices they offer you.

It really can be an effective way of improving the relationship between you and your supplier and lead to a substantial reduction in costs. A *Supplier Day* is definitely worth a try!

CHAPTER SUMMARY

- *Your supplier needs you just as much as you need them*

- *Work together to make the "right" profit*

- *It is all about give and take*

- *Organise a Supplier Day*

- *Encourage your supplier to help you out*

- *Let your supplier buy from you*

- *Ask for 'inside' tips*

Chapter Ten

WORKING WITH US

I had always been set on calling this book *Using Less Stuff!* even though a few friends and colleagues were ambivalent about my choice of title. One said, *"It's a great name, but why don't you chop off the 'stuff' and keep it as Using Less?"* another suggested, *"How about Less is More?"* Both would have been fine names. Their concern was that *Using Less Stuff!* might come across as too informal for a book that wants to be taken seriously. For me, this impression of seriousness was something to be apprehensive about.

As I see it, many books that talk about social responsibility often highlight the seriousness and importance of the subject and risk coming across as sanctimonious. I find that tone tends to put people off. The message I want to get across is straightforward; it doesn't need dressing up. Cost reduction is really just about using less stuff.

We all – as individuals, schools and businesses – have *stuff.* We all love *having* stuff, *using* stuff, buying *new* stuff, selling *old* stuff, even sometimes *sharing* stuff. Unfortunately, it just so happens that we all want to use *more* stuff, while at the same time all the stuff around us is running out. The big question is: Can we *afford* to use so much stuff?

In this book, I set out to demonstrate one thing.

I wanted to show that there are countless, easy ways to save large amounts of money simply by **USING LESS STUFF**. And, what's more, the effects will be dramatic and long lasting.

In general it is an enormous struggle getting people excited about social responsibility, but the truth is there for everyone to see: the population is rapidly increasing and resources are becoming scarcer. Now, this is quite a terrifying thought. It's overwhelming because it's such a huge problem and, when seen as facts and figures, graphs and tables, it can seem opaque and abstracted from your day-to-day reality. The sceptic might ask: *Why should I save the planet when no one else is doing anything about it?*

So, I think pushing the doom and gloom aspect is the wrong approach. All I want to do is get across a simple message, something direct and useful. Let's reframe the sceptic's question to make it more personal. How about asking, instead: *Why is it relevant to me? How does it affect my school, my business?*

The answer to these questions is straightforward: using less stuff will save you money!

And with the government's *Carbon Reduction Commitment* launching its phases 2 and 3, which target smaller businesses, you cannot afford to ignore this. Schools and businesses will need to answer for high levels of consumption.

So, where to start with cost reduction? There are lots of things you can do first; it doesn't really matter as long as you do something **NOW!** You must take action; your costs won't reduce themselves!

The first thing to note is that cost reduction is a proactive task, not a reactive one. Most schools and businesses already have their hands full dealing with more immediate issues than reducing costs.

Therefore, outsourcing may be the best option for you. This will let you focus on your core business, while the experts save you money.

At *The Cost Reduction Company*, we are currently promoting *Using Less,* an initiative aimed at both saving schools money by reducing consumption and teaching the pupils about social responsibility. If you prefer to conduct your own cost reduction programme then you should begin with measurement. Only when you know what you are using now, can you start working out how to start using less. Once you have a complete assessment of where you are wasting money and who is responsible, you can draw up a plan on how to prevent this and educate your staff about reducing their usage.

Measurement is just the start; you need a system in place that continually monitors your usage. Keeping on top of things is essential.

Never forget that cost reduction is a team game. You need to tackle these issues as a whole, from the bottom to the top of your organisation. Everyone needs to be involved. Everyone must be held accountable for any unnecessary usage. If your organisation is a school, then this means getting the governors, the head, the bursars, the teachers, the non-teaching staff, the children and the parents involved. If you have a business, this means encouraging all of your staff to come up with cost-cutting ideas and creating an atmosphere where they feel confident that their ideas will be heard.

The CEO or Head needs to take responsibility for the project. Always keep asking questions like: *Why are we doing it this way? Are there any cheaper alternatives?*

You need to get rid of the *"Because we always have!"* attitude and keep everyone continually questioning and improving on their day-to-day tasks.

Another great tip is to look for quick wins to prove how easy it is to make savings.

Excellent communication is vital. For instance, many employees won't know that they are wasting resources. You can alter consumption by ironing out bad habits.

It is important to note that savings can be found anywhere, and that any small saving will add up to a larger whole. Once a saving is made, you will benefit from making it for years to come.

When it comes to specification, make sure that all parties involved are clear about what is going on and what is expected from them.

This is all down to communication. It is about taking the time to ask the right questions. You can reduce costs by being more specific about your needs.

Make sure you involve your suppliers, the manufacturers and the end user. Think about organising a *Supplier Day*. An excellent specification will guarantee control over your business.

Also, there is a whole lot more to reducing costs than seeking out cheaper alternatives to your current pricing. Cheap goods are usually cheap for a reason. What you want is value!

What it all boils down to is, why would you want to waste money when you don't have to?

If you can run your business for 15% less than what it's currently costing and it doesn't affect your performance in terms of what you are delivering – services and quality – you can use these extra savings to drive the business forward. It gives you the choice to spend that 15% on whatever you want, rather than on unnecessary costs.

We all make mistakes – the real mistake is to keep making them!

INDEX

ABOUT THE AUTHOR

Nigel Ward has over 30 years experience working in business. After five years in the Army he worked as a Retail Director in *Allied Breweries*, working for *Taylor Walker* in London and *Tetley Walker* in Liverpool.

He then set up a consultancy in the leisure industry and helped develop several well-known brands including *Pitcher & Piano Bars*. It was in this capacity that he sharpened his skills in cost-reduction.

Nigel started *The Cost Reduction Company* four years ago to help businesses, especially schools, reduce their day-to-day running costs and consumption. This was after identifying that finance departments were becoming more and more stretched and had less time to look at how to reduce their usage in the long-term.

He developed long-term cost reduction processes and a sustainable programme for consumption reduction called *Using Less*. This has become the key direction for his business as the concept has grown.

He targets the education sector and has built up a strong following in that field, as schools need to combine cost savings with long-term sustainable savings.

Nigel's clients include *Oxford* and *Cambridge University Colleges* and large public schools including *Eton, Bradfield* and *Malvern*. He has also worked regularly in the fast-growing Academy sector. He has worked with *NHS Hospitals*, Lords Cricket Ground and several well-known hotel chains.

Nigel has a large family of five children and is very keen on sports. He can be regularly found at *Lords* where he is a member. He is still active on the cricket field and plays golf and tennis.

You can contact *The Cost Reduction Company* at:

www.thecostreductioncompany.co.uk
save@thecostreductioncompany.co.uk

Newtown House
Newtown Road
Henley-on-Thames
Oxon RG9 1HG

+44 (0) 1491 637377

USING LESS STUFF

Lightning Source UK Ltd.
Milton Keynes UK
UKOW04f2141120514

231562UK00021B/890/P